# A Little Book

of

# English Saints

by

Simon Webb

Published by the Langley Press, 2016



The front cover shows a picture of Edward the Confessor (left) with Edward the Martyr (?) from British Library Manuscript Royal 2 B VI, an illuminated book of psalms and canticles made at St Albans in the middle of the thirteenth century. All the pictures in this book are public domain images from books in the British Library: www.bl.uk

Also from the Langley Press:

In Search of the Northern Saints
The Legend of Saint Cuthbert
In Search of Saint Alban
The History of King Richard III by Thomas More
In Search of Bede
The Theology of Small Things
The Voyage of Saint Brendan
Bede's Life of Saint Cuthbert
Gilbert's Tale: The Life and
Death of Thomas Becket
Nicholas Breakspear: The Pope from England

For free downloads and more from the Langley Press, visit our website at http://tinyurl.com/lpdirect

# Contents

*St George: From BL Harley MS 2900, France, C15th*

# Introduction

Hagiographies, or lives of the saints, used to be very popular reading, at least among the Christian countries of western Europe. Books like *The Golden Legend*, a collection of hagiographies written by Jacobus de Voragine, were the medieval equivalents of best-sellers: over a thousand manuscripts of Jacobus's work have survived.

In later centuries, popular books about saints included John Foxe's *Acts and Monuments*, known as *Foxe's Book of Martyrs*, which was first published in 1563, and went through four editions in Foxe's own life-time.

Foxe wrote from a Protestant, anti-Catholic point of view, but his most popular successor was Alban Butler, an English eighteenth-century Catholic priest, whose multi-volume *Lives of the Saints* remains a valuable reference-book for anyone interested in the subject.

The popularity of saints' lives has declined together with the declining influence of Churches of many Christian denominations; but a lack of knowledge of the lives of these remarkable people is a disadvantage for anyone with an interest in the history of the Christian centuries, and the cultures of the countries that are now regarded as post-Christian. Anyone who fails to read any saints' lives is also missing out on some terrific stories.

The fact that miracles, some of them entertainingly outlandish, feature in large numbers in many saints' lives, is off-putting for some people, who suspect that the hagiographer is somehow trying to dupe them into becoming devotees by using the hypnotic power of a series of tall tales. Such a response shows a failure to understand the purpose of many hagiographies, which were written not to carry that elusive cargo called 'what actually happened', but to bring the reader glimpses of the nature and power of the divine. When there is a possibility of conveying that kind of spiritual insight, some authors, particularly in the medieval period, threw considerations such as plausibility out of the window.

From the modern perspective, the resulting literature can be classified as a type of mythology. Mythology involves myths, of course, and, although we might read ancient pagan myths for their entertainment value, there is no getting away from the fact that the best and most enduring ones have important things to say, not just about the culture that spawned them, but about the human condition everywhere, and at all times. This is why, for instance, the Greek myth of Antigone has been used in modern management training courses, and the myth of Oedipus is of interest not only to students of ancient Greek literature, but also to followers of Freudian psycho-analysis.

The miraculous and 'mythological' content of the following saints' lives, which are arranged in chronological order, tends to diminish as the period in which the saint lived grows closer to our own. Its place is taken by more fine-grained historical detail. But the sources on which the following versions are based were written by authors for whom the warm glow of the spirit mattered as much, if not more, than the cold light that lays everything bare, but reveals nothing of abiding interest.

*The martyrdoms of St Alban (top) and St Amphibalus, BL Royal MS 2 B VI, England, C13th*

# I. Alban

One day around the year 303 AD, the emperor Diocletian tried to look into the future. One technique used by the pagan Romans to see what time had in store for them relied on the work of the so-called 'haruspices'; fortune-tellers who gazed, not into crystal balls or the bottoms of tea-cups, but at the internal organs of freshly-killed farm animals.

According to Lactantius, a Christian author who lived at the same time as Diocletian, the emperor favoured a form of haruspicy called hepatomancy. In this version, the soothsayers looked closely at the livers of the sacrificial victims, hoping to spot a blemish or abnormality that could be taken as a clue from the gods, about what was lurking around time's corner.

On that fateful day around 303, Diocletian's hepatomancers found neither terrifying nor reassuring signs on the livers they examined. In fact they found nothing at all – the livers were disappointingly healthy and normal.

Worried that his personal supply of messages

from the gods had been cut off, the emperor asked the soothsayers for an explanation. Their leader, a man called Tages, told Diocletian that he was being denied his view of futurity because 'profane persons' were present at the hepatomancers' ceremonies. These 'profane persons' turned out to be Christians who worked for the emperor, and were in the habit of making the sign of the cross on their own foreheads, much as some Christians today will make the sign over their chests.

Tages' words implied that, by making the sign of the cross, the Christians were blocking the pagan gods' ability to alter the livers of the sacrificial victims. The Christian author Lactantius had his own theory, however: he said the Christians were scaring off the demons who usually did the job. This shows how the Christians of those days, like the Jews of Old Testament times, tended to think pagan gods were demons in disguise.

Diocletian responded to this intolerable situation by declaring that all his staff should immediately prove that they were not Christians, by sacrificing to the Roman gods. If they refused to do so, they would be whipped. The emperor went further, and insisted that all the soldiers who worked for him should sacrifice, or be dismissed from the army.

These actions of the emperor did not add up to anything like a full-scale persecution; but

Diocletian was persuaded to up the stakes by his son-in-law Caesar Galerius. Galerius's mother had long held a grudge against the Christians, which had to do with what happened to the bodies of the sacrificial animals after the haruspices had finished with them. Galerius's mother was in the habit of serving up meat from these animals at her dinner-parties. Because they knew the source of this meat, the local Christians always turned down her dinner invitations.

Galerius and his mother, who may have been called Romula, persuaded Diocletian to unleash what became known as the Great Persecution, in which many Christians perished throughout the Roman empire.

According to some sources, it was during Diocletian's persecution that St George, long the patron saint of England, was killed for his Christian beliefs.

We are told that as soon as he heard about the emperor's actions against his fellow-Christians, George, who was an officer in the Roman army, went to Diocletian and confessed to him that he was, indeed, a Christian. The emperor offered him land, money and slaves, if only he would sacrifice to the pagan gods; but George refused.

What happened next has been so heavily embroidered by re-tellers of the story that it has become ludicrous, and the core of truth in the tale, if there is one, may now be lost forever. Some write of him being tortured on a wheel of knives, and then beheaded. Other accounts say that George's body was chopped up, that he was buried alive, and then burned alive, in that order, and that each time, he came back to life. At last, decapitation seemed the only option, but the executioners found that milk, and not blood, flowed from George's severed neck.

If it is true that George perished under Diocletian, then although Diocletian was indeed the Roman emperor, it is unlikely that England's patron saint was killed in Rome itself. Diocletian had made the eastern city of Nicomedia his capital: the site of this city is in the north-west of Anatolia, the oblong expanse of land that makes up most of modern Turkey.

Before he got round to killing George, Diocletian began his persecution of the Christians by ordering the destruction of the Christian church in Nicomedia: thereafter the empire's widespread, nerve-like system of communications pushed the persecution out to the far corners of the Roman world.

An outpost of Rome that was nearly two and a half thousand miles from Nicomedia, and over twelve hundred miles from Rome itself, was Britain. This remote set of islands had started to become part of the Roman empire two centuries before Diocletian was born, and by the time the Great Persecution reached our shores, there were thriving Roman towns and cities in many areas of what later became England.

One of the cities of Roman Britain was Verulamium, now St Albans in Hertfordshire, which lies some twenty-four miles to the north-west of London. There one of the citizens, a man named Alban, became a Christian and was martyred for his faith in a very short space of time.

As the persecution raged through Britain, Alban sheltered a Christian fugitive in his own house in the city. Impressed by the man's piety and devotion, Alban himself became a Christian; but soon word reached the local magistrate that Alban was harbouring the fugitive.

When the soldiers came to Alban's door, they found no trace of the man Alban had been protecting: instead they discovered the protector himself, dressed in the fugitive's clothes. By substituting himself for his new friend, the saint was following the teaching of Jesus in the Gospel of John (15:13). Here Christ tells us that 'Greater love hath no man than this, that a man lay down his life for his friends' (King James Version).

Alban was dragged before the magistrate, who threatened to inflict on him the punishment he had been planning to use on Alban's new friend. The saint was unmoved by these threats, and refused to give any information about himself beyond his name. He also refused to sacrifice to pagan idols, and said that by continuing to sacrifice to the ‘demons’, the magistrate himself was guaranteeing his own place in hell.

The magistrate, now furious, condemned Alban to be beheaded. It was during the process of his execution that Alban performed all the miracles he was responsible for in life; but like many saints, his miracles also continued long after his death.

Alban was sentenced to be executed outside the city of Verulamium, beside a river. As he approached the place, no doubt flanked by guards, the saint saw that almost the entire population of the city had turned out to see his execution. Many of them were packed onto the bridge over the river, and there was no way for Alban and his guards to get across. At the edge of the water, Alban said a prayer, and the river instantly dried up, so that he could be led across. This miracle impressed one member of the party very much: this was the man who had been detailed to behead Alban. Suddenly converted to Christianity, and filled with a new insight into who and what his intended victim was, the executioner threw down his sword. The new convert, who is described as a soldier, was martyred straight after Alban.

At the top of a nearby hill, ‘enamelled with a great variety of flowers, or rather quite covered with them’, a substitute swordsman struck off Alban’s head, though not before the saint had caused a spring of water to appear, to quench his thirst. At the moment when Alban’s head was parted from his body, the eyes of the stand-in executioner popped out of their sockets and fell to the ground. Hearing about this collection of miracles, the magistrate who had condemned Alban went on to do his best to stop the deadly operation of the Great Persecution in Britain.

The account of Alban's martyrdom printed above contains all the important incidents concerning Alban related by the Venerable Bede in his *Ecclesiastical History of the English People*, which was completed around 731 AD.

Bede was a remarkable man – a Northumbrian monk, priest, historian and scientist, who went to great lengths to base his *Ecclesiastical History* on the most reliable sources. He includes Alban in his history partly because the man from Verulamium is the first known Christian martyr of England.

Despite his importance, and the status Alban conferred on St Albans, the city that was later named after him, Bede actually gives us very little information on the so-called '*protomartyr Anglorum*'.

Bede does give us a vague idea of when Alban's martyrdom happened (during the persecution of Diocletian) and he also gives us a calendar date – the twenty-second of June. But he does not tell us the name of the magistrate who condemned Alban, or of the soldier who refused to kill the saint, or the man who eventually did the deed and was blinded for his pains. Bede does not even supply the name of the original Christian fugitive whom Alban sheltered.

Bede has an opportunity to supply some of Alban's back-story when the magistrate asks him about his family, but the saint refuses to give any details beyond his name. It is clear that the magistrate has no prior knowledge of Alban, and we have no clue from Bede about Alban's occupation or status in the community. We also do not learn whether Alban was a Briton or a Roman (or a combination of the two), how old he was, what he looked like, or whether he was a native of Verulamium, or had been born somewhere else. We know that he had his own house, and Bede implies that he was a virgin (so we can perhaps discount a wife and children) but beyond that, Bede's Alban is rather mysterious. We are not even told how much time elapsed between the martyr's first meeting with his Christian guest, and his own execution.

Given Alban's unique status as the English protomartyr, it is perhaps inevitable that succeeding generations should have grown dissatisfied with the lack of detail in Bede's account. Re-tellers of the story, including the fifteenth-century poet John Lydgate, added to the narrative, turning Bede's plain but sturdy chair, as it were, into an elaborate throne, with intricate carving and lavish gilding.

In his long narrative poem on St Alban, Lydgate, a monk of Bury St Edmunds, gave names to the saint's Christian guest ('Amphibalus'), and also to the magistrate who condemned him, and the soldier who refused to behead him. He also gave Alban the status of a kind of princely viceroy of Britain, who usually wore a cloak fringed with gold, which he swapped for the grotty old cloak of Amphibalus, the Christian fugitive.

Lydgate also supplies an elaborate prequel to the tale of Alban's martyrdom, relating an important journey to Rome, some interaction with the emperor, and even a previous meeting with Amphibalus.

Whereas Bede's story may cover only a few days, Lydgate makes it clear that several months passed between Amphibalus's entry into Verulamium, and the death of his saintly protector. Lydgate even adds to the miracles surrounding Alban's martyrdom, telling us how several spectators drowned in the river after they had fallen off the overcrowded bridge, but were brought back to life after Alban caused the river to dry up.

In a detail that resembles an element in the story of St George, the magistrate offers Alban great wealth and extensive lands, if only he will sacrifice to the pagan gods.

The eye-catching but sometimes wild and indiscriminate embroidery that is often applied to saints' lives can be a stumbling-block for anyone trying to find the 'definitive' version of the life of, for instance, St Cuthbert. A multiplicity of different accounts can also be a problem: this is particularly true in the case of Thomas Becket. Elements that seem central to one version of the life of a saint can be entirely missing from another account, and readers familiar with one version may not be able to recognise the saint described in another, although he or she is supposed to be the same person.

In the case of Alban, the questions of whether he ever really existed, and whether he perished under Diocletian, or under some other persecuting emperor, also have to be seriously considered.

It is possible that Alban was a victim of another Roman emperor, called Decius, whose persecution of Christians began some fifty years before Diocletian's. As we will see when we come to the life of Edward the Confessor, Decius was responsible for a particularly wicked crime against seven brave Christians outside the city of Ephesus (now also in Turkey). These Christians had hidden in a cave, and when they were found there, fast asleep, Decius ordered that they should be sealed in, so that they could never escape.

After comparing different versions of saints' lives, it is tempting to suspect that the elaborators of these stories, such as John Lydgate, were liars and show-offs, and that their overlong accounts obscure the true nature of the relevant saint. As has already been intimated in the introduction to this book, this would be to misunderstand the status and purpose of those old hagiographers. Their definition of the word ‘truth’, and their motivation for writing history and biography would have been quite different from those of most modern writers. It is clear that part of Lydgate’s reason for writing at such length about Alban was to use the saint’s story to bring out some of the central ideas of Christianity as he understood it. Likewise, Bede, in his introduction, actually states that he wants the reader of his *Ecclesiastical History* to be a better Christian after he or she has read it, to embrace virtuous examples, and to avoid the ways of the wicked. I suspect that a modern writer might lose the trust of his or her readers if he or she stated such a goal at the beginning of some new historical work.

We might include among the possible objectives of Bede, and later English chroniclers, a patriotic determination to present Britain, stranded as it is off the extreme edge of Europe, as a place with a noble and eventful history, imbued with the Christian spirit from the earliest possible times: a place where saints could spring up, and miracles be performed.

Unfortunately, some of those old writers of the lives of the saints had less worthy motivations in mind than patriotism, or the promotion of faith and virtue, when they sat down to write. Matthew

Paris, the thirteenth-century monk and chronicler, recounted the story of Little St Hugh of Lincoln, a bizarre tale of ritual murder fabricated to spur the reader to furious anti-Semitism. Likewise, in his *History of the Church of Durham,* the twelfth century chronicler Simeon of Durham went out of his way to give very detailed accounts of all the lands granted to his local diocese, no doubt to 'firm up' the said diocese's claim to those lands.

According to Lydgate's version of the life of Alban, the saint is able to recognise Amphibalus as a Christian when he first meets him in Verulamium, although he knows practically nothing about Christianity, except that he has evidently been told that it is something to be avoided.

This doesn't quite fit with another story, from Bede, concerning St Lucius, who was a king of the Britons in the middle of the second century A.D. Lucius the royal saint is also mentioned by Geoffrey of Monmouth, the twelfth century chronicler.

According to Geoffrey, Lucius, who may have lived over a century and a half before Alban, sat down and wrote a letter to the then pope, Eleutherius, in Rome. In his letter, the king begged the pontiff to send him missionaries to convert the British to Christianity. Lucius had heard tales of the miracles performed by Christian missionaries in other parts of the world, and he wanted to connect himself and his kingdom with this wonderful new faith.

Eleutherius sent Faganus and Duvianus as missionaries to Lucius's court, and soon the king had been taught about Christianity, and baptised. Many of his subjects followed his example, and Faganus and Duvianus set about converting the local pagan priests (called flamens) into Christian priests, bishops and archbishops. Eventually, the two missionaries returned to Rome, but were soon back with more missionaries in attendance, to mop up the last remnants of British paganism. Under Lucius and his successors, Britain remained Christian until the time of the emperor Diocletian, under whom Alban is said to have perished. Lucius set an example for later Christian kings and other magnates by granting large tracts of land to the church.

Although Alban is recognised as the first English martyr for Christianity, Lucius must count among our first saints. He was both a saint and a king – something that was to become quite common as the Christian centuries rolled over England. Other famous kingly saints of England include Oswald of Northumbria, Sigeberht of the East Angles, and Edward the Confessor.

It may be that, despite his crucial role in the introduction of the Christian faith into Britain, Lucius is not well-known because his story, as related by Bede and Geoffrey, is rather smooth and undramatic. The transition from ancient paganism to the new faith seems to have gone without a hitch, and Bede records no revolts or even complaints against the introduction of Christianity, even from the powerful flamens.

It is difficult to reconcile the supposed widespread Christianisation of Britain under Lucius with Alban's initial ignorance of the essentials of Christianity, as described by John Lydgate. If we take Lydgate at face value, we might have to suppose that, like many of those early, legendary kings of Britain, Lucius's kingdom was limited to only a small portion of these islands, which did not include Alban's city of Verulamium. Lucius's kingdom, if it ever really existed, may have been a Christian enclave surrounded by pagan powers. In the later, Anglo-Saxon period, such kingdoms existed, and their rulers sometimes felt compelled to wage war against their heathen neighbours.

The story of King Lucius and his letter to the pope hints at the existence of Christianity in at least part of Britain long before Alban; but another twelfth century chronicler, William of Malmesbury, reminds us that the Word may have reached these islands even earlier than Lucius. William tells us that while the pope's missionaries Faganus and Duvianus were in Britain, they paid a visit to Glastonbury, then an island, but now a place well inland in the modern English county of Somerset. There they found the remains of a church that was over a hundred years old.

William tells us that Faganus and Duvianus remained at Glastonbury for nine years. They researched the history of the place 'in ancient writings' and discovered that the church had been built by twelve disciples of Jesus, only thirty years or so after their master's crucifixion. These disciples included Joseph of Arimathea, who had organised the burial of Jesus after the crucifixion, arranging for Christ's body to be placed in his own recently-prepared tomb.

Joseph and his eleven companions had been sent to Britain by St Philip, who had worked hard to convert the people across the English Channel in what we now call France. We are told that Philip regarded Joseph of Arimathea as his best friend. The island where they settled, which was 'surrounded by woods and thickets and marshes' was given to them by a local pagan king. Two more kings also granted them land, though the kings themselves refused to adopt the Christian religion. The angel Gabriel ordered the holy immigrants to build their humble church, and they dedicated it to the Virgin Mary.

This early Christian mission to Britain, based at Glastonbury, was something of a historical dead end, since after the twelve disciples died, 'the place became a lair of wild beasts'. But when Faganus and Duvianus re-discovered it, they restored the old church, built a second church, and founded a monastic community consisting of twelve men. This small monastery continued to operate in its original form for over three hundred years, until, according to some accounts, St Patrick, apostle of the Irish, settled there, with some Irish brethren, and revived and re-organised the community.

An old document called *The Charter of St Patrick the Bishop* tells us that Patrick promised great spiritual benefits to anyone who helped with the heavy task of clearing the trees off the island, which was known as Yniswitrin. Another name for it is Avalon.

*Saint Cuthbert and King Ecgfrith, from BL Yates Thompson MS 26, English, C12th*

## II. Cuthbert

Most English people have heard of the river Tyne that flows between the cities of Newcastle and Gateshead, and is spanned by many majestic bridges. Few, however, are aware of the existence of the Scottish river Tyne, which rises south of Edinburgh, and flows north-east until it empties itself into the North Sea near Belhaven, on the western shoulder of Scotland.

It was on this more modest, northerly Tyne that a terrible tragedy was averted, some time around the middle of the seventh century AD.

Some monks had founded a monastery on the south bank of the river, near the point where it joins the sea. Bede, the eighth-century Northumbrian chronicler, tells us that the monks would fetch any timber they needed from the woods upriver, and float it down to their monastery on rafts.

One day, while this risky operation was underway, a strong wind appeared from nowhere and, just as a small fleet of five rafts was nearing its landing-place, it was blown right past, and seemed to be bound for the open ocean. In his biography of Saint Cuthbert, Bede adds the detail that the rafts were soon so far off that they looked like five tiny birds on the surface of the water.

Some attempt was made by monks on the river-bank to get hold of the rafts before they had blown too far away – one can picture monks in unsuitable heavy woollen habits wading into the river – but the wind and the waves got the better of them, and soon the rafts were out of reach.

By now the monks had all poured out of their monastery buildings, and were praying for their endangered brothers, while sheltering from the weather behind a large rock. On the north side of the river a crowd of rubber-necked peasants had gathered to watch events unfold. They certainly did not pray for the monks on the stricken rafts, as their brothers on land were doing. They cursed them, ridiculed their way of life, said they hoped that God would not help them, and complained that nobody understood their new religion anyway.

A future saint called Cuthbert was standing among the peasants, and he scolded them for their wickedness. Shouldn't you pray for those poor fellows? he asked. Seeing that they would not, Cuthbert, who was probably only a teenager at the time, knelt down to pray for them himself. At once, the wind changed direction, and gently pushed the raft-borne monks back to their landing-place.

Abashed, the mocking peasants, who were evidently still pagans in their hearts, gained a new respect for Cuthbert, and became good Christians on the spot.

The story of the near-tragedy on the Scottish Tyne is like one of those half-remembered childhood recollections that give up more details the more you think about them.

The most striking detail is the pagan-hearted peasants who curse the stricken monks, simply because they, the monks, are Christians, and are living in a monastic community. In Bede's account, the peasants blame the monks for abandoning ordinary life and living according to a Rule that, clearly, seemed newfangled to some English people at that time. Bede's peasants also accuse the monks of having abandoned the old, pagan ways of worship, and having embraced an incomprehensible new religion. The life of Cuthbert, and of many of the so-called Northern Saints who lived around his time, was lived near the very beginning of Christianity among the English, as opposed to the British.

As we have seen, Christianity had come to the British, and the Roman Britons, centuries earlier; but the Anglo-Saxon invaders who pushed the Britons into the west, and gave their name to England, were originally pagans. The remains of the Germanic type of paganism that the Anglo-

Saxons brought with them can still be found in the English names for the days of the week: Wednesday was named for the god Woden, Thursday for Thor, etc.

The fact that the peasants in the story above were at best half-hearted Christians may be a result of the method by which the people of England were, in theory, converted to Christianity.

In Northumbria, the Anglo-Saxon kingdom with which St Cuthbert is associated, the Word had come via St Oswald, one of those celebrated saintly kings of these islands, who invited Celtic Christian missionaries from Iona, which lies off the opposite, western side of Scotland from the Scottish Tyne (if Scotland can be said to have a shoulder, then Iona is part of Scotland's moustache).

Although biographies of St Aidan, the most celebrated of King Oswald's missionaries, tend to insist that he brought his message to all the people, the scepticism of those riverside peasants would seem to suggest that, though the nobles took to Jesus, Christian ideas didn't always trickle down to the ordinary folk.

The fact that Cuthbert's Christianity contrasted with the ideas of the peasants whose words so shocked him is one of several clues that suggest that this saint came from an aristocratic background.

Another interesting feature of Bede's story is

that his monks clearly possessed a skill-set which included the capabilities of the modern lumberjack: the ability to select and cut down suitable timber, and transport it on river-borne rafts. By contrast, in some monastic orders, this sort of work was done by lay workers – employees of the monastery – while the monks themselves filled their time with prayer, study and contemplation. As we shall see, Cuthbert himself had many practical skills, including the ability to put up sturdy buildings single-handed, and also to grow crops in very unpromising conditions.

Although Cuthbert was raised as a Christian by his saintly foster-mother Kenswith, he was brought to a more direct and serious religious attitude by a vision he had one night while tending some sheep on the northern hills. (The fact that Cuthbert was raised by a foster-mother is another indication that he came from a noble family.)

While his companions slept, Cuthbert had stayed awake to pray. Looking up, he saw light streaming down from heaven. The streams of light contained angels, who came down to gather up the glowing soul of the aforementioned St Aidan, who had died that night.

The sudden strengthening of Cuthbert's faith that followed his vision made him seek out a nearby monastery in which to start a new life. The site of the ruins of Old Melrose Abbey is only forty miles or so south-west from the place where

Cuthbert's prayers changed the wind-direction and saved the lumberjack monks. It was here that Cuthbert, having given the sheep he had been tending back to their owners, began his monastic training.

It is an important detail of the story that Cuthbert arrived at Melrose on a horse, carrying a spear. Only a nobleman could have done that at the time, since neither horses nor spears were owned by the peasantry. St Boisil, who was then prior of Melrose, happened to be standing at the door as Cuthbert arrived, and he welcomed the young man warmly. He immediately recognised his piety, quoting Jesus as he said, 'Behold an Israelite indeed, in whom is no guile' (John 1:47). Later, when as an old man he was dying of the plague, Boisil prophesied to Cuthbert that he, Cuthbert, would become a bishop.

Standing with Boisil when Cuthbert first arrived at Melrose was one Sigfrith, then a boy, whom Bede knew as an elderly priest. Such 'living histories', old people who had witnessed past events, were among Bede's sources for his biography of Cuthbert.

Cuthbert suffered from the plague that killed Boisil, but he recovered, and Prior Boisil made another prophesy, that he would never suffer from it again. On Boisil's death, Cuthbert became prior, and he set about repairing the damage the plague had done to the faith of the lay people in the area.

In their desperation, the locals had turned away from Jesus, back to idols and pagan amulets, as they had watched their families die. Cuthbert was tireless in seeking out remote communities in the hills, and trying to re-connect them with Christianity.

As well as the peasantry, the local monks and nuns also benefited from Cuthbert's inspired teaching. Aebbe, the abbess of Coldingham, which is just a few miles east of the mouth of the Scottish Tyne, asked Cuthbert to visit. While he was there, one of the monks noticed that their visitor was in the habit of leaving his bed and spending all night somewhere else. The monk followed him, down to the sea, where Cuthbert waded in until the water was up to his neck. There, he prayed all night, and when he returned to the beach, sea-otters came and warmed and dried his feet with their breath and their fur.

The incident involving the sea-otters is not the only story about Cuthbert that involves animals. In England, where the people have a great affection for their native creatures, Cuthbert's connection with them has helped endear the saint to many.

One day, while the saint was travelling in a wild, remote area with a small boy, his companion started to panic because there seemed to be no hope of them getting anything to eat in the foreseeable future. As if on cue, an eagle delivered a fresh fish. True to his nature, Cuthbert insisted that the eagle should have its own share of the fish.

Unlike his version of the story of St Alban, which may be intended to cover only a few days of action, Bede's biography of St Cuthbert follows the saint's whole life – a period of over fifty years. Like many hagiographies, Cuthbert's contains many stories of miracles, some of which seem to be very much in the style of the miracles of Jesus. Like Jesus, Cuthbert took part in miraculous events involving bread, and healed a woman who was possessed by a demon that made her behave rather like Legion, the madman of Gadara in the gospels. Another demon-possessed individual in the gospels is the daughter of the woman from Canaan, whom Jesus healed although he had never even seen her. The possessed woman Cuthbert cured, the wife of a man called Hildmer, was also cured long-distance, and was found to be well by the time Cuthbert came to visit her.

Bede insists that, quite apart from his work as a maker of miracles, Cuthbert was an exemplary monk, priest, and prior; but despite his success as a monastic leader, the saint sought the solitude of the hermit's life. He retired to the island of Inner Farne, just over a mile off the coast of Northumbria, where the shoulder of Scotland becomes the upper back of England. The island itself is roughly diamond-shaped, and measures less than a third of a mile across at its widest point. There, surrounded by rocks and sea-birds, Cuthbert built himself a house, a chapel and a guest-house for visitors, with walls made up of stones and peat.

Before he could begin his construction work, he had to drive the devil and his followers from the island. Then the coast was clear for angels to come and assist Cuthbert with his building projects. With a combination of prayer and help from some visiting monks, the saint also managed to dig a well, that soon filled up with fresh water.

After a failed attempt to grow wheat, Cuthbert managed to raise barley on Inner Farne. He also succeeded in keeping birds from stealing his crops and pilfering his thatch to build their own nests, by commanding them to desist, in God's name.

It seems, however, that the devils that had once inhabited the place would sometimes return and do battle with the man Bede calls 'God's soldier'. They would hurl stones at him, try to throw him off cliffs, and tempt him with strange visions.

Cuthbert may have stayed on his island for as many as nine years before he was elected bishop of Lindisfarne in his absence, at a synod held in the presence of Ecgfrith, king of Northumbria. The semi-island of Lindisfarne was then home to a monastery, which had been founded by the aforementioned St Aidan. Close to Bambrugh, the stronghold of the Northumbria kings, Lindisfarne was the focal-point of Northumbrian Christianity at the time.

In true saintly fashion, Cuthbert was reluctant

to leave his island and take on the responsibilities of a bishopric. At last he consented, after King Ecgfrith, accompanied by Bishop Trumwine of the Picts and an impressive selection of the great and the good, sailed to Cuthbert's island and begged him to come back with them. This incident is illustrated in a picture in a gorgeous twelfth-century manuscript edition of Bede's Life of Cuthbert, now known as British Library Yates Thompson Manuscript 26. Here the saint is seen in his severe black habit, at the door of his little DIY house, shaking the hand of Ecgfrith, who simultaneously wags a finger of royal command at him.

Bede insists that, despite his many years of solitude, Cuthbert adapted well to his new role as a bishop though, like Edward the Confessor centuries later, he managed to maintain a saintly life during his years of power.

He turned water into wine, spoke prophesies, saw visions, performed many miracles of the healing variety, and continued to travel to remote places to preach to the people. Some of his healing miracles restored people who were very close to death (for instance from the plague) to full health. As in the case of Hildmer's wife, it wasn't always necessary for Cuthbert to visit the sick to heal them. Holy water sent from him, or bread blessed by him, would sometimes do just as well.

But it seems that Cuthbert himself had not been

well for some time. One of his prophesies concerned his own imminent death, and after only two years as bishop of Lindisfarne, he returned to his hermitage on Inner Farne.

As Cuthbert's final illness took hold, a visiting priest called Herefrith found the saint lying helpless on his rudimentary bed, chewing on raw onions to take away his hunger and thirst. He said he wanted to be buried there, alone on his island, but the monks begged their bishop to allow them to bury him in their church. This they did, but after his death the saint continued to perform miracles. Even soil onto which water had been thrown away, which had been used to wash Cuthbert's dead body, had the power to cure a local boy who was possessed by a ferocious demon.

Cuthbert's corpse slept to the right of the altar in St Peter's church on Lindisfarne for eleven years, until something inspired the monks to open his tomb and have a look at him. They were shocked to find him looking as if he had just gone to sleep. After all those years, his limbs were still flexible, and his grave-clothes were fresh and fragrant. The state of his body, found to be 'incorrupt', was taken as a sure sign that Cuthbert was a saint.

Over a century later, Cuthbert's rest was disturbed again, but this time the disruption could not be blamed on the curiosity of the local monks. In the summer of 793 AD the north-east of

England was raided by what we call Vikings – people the old chroniclers tended to refer to as Danes. The 793 attack has gone down in history as the first recorded Viking attack on Europe. As described by the twelfth-century chronicler Simeon of Durham, the raid was brutal and shocking. The local churches were 'miserably filled with blood, and rapine, and all but entirely and thoroughly ruined'. The pagan raiders 'slew not only the cattle, but even the priests and deacons, and the choirs of monks and nuns'. When they reached Lindisfarne itself, on the seventh of June, 'they miserably ravaged and pillaged everything; they trod the holy things under their polluted feet, they dug down the altars, and plundered all the treasures of the church. Some of the brethren they slew, some they carried off with them in chains, the greater number they stripped naked, insulted, and cast out of doors, and some they drowned in the sea'.

Although the sacking of Lindisfarne was indeed shocking, it was not entirely unexpected. The people of Northumbria had been expecting disaster for some time. A series of spectacular storms, featuring 'fearful thunders and fiery dragons flying through the sky' had alerted them to the possibility that very bad news was on its way.

Despite the severity of this raid, which, if nothing else, must have made the monks who later repopulated Lindisfarne horribly aware of the vulnerability of their island to a sea-borne attack, it was not until over eighty years later, in 875, that the then bishop, Eardulf, decided to quit Lindisfarne altogether.

It may be that when the monks who had survived the raid of 793 conducted a post-mortem on recent events among the ruins of their ravaged community, they decided that the recent raids had been opportunistic ones: a kind of large-scale armed robbery. But the reappearance of the Vikings on British soil in the middle of the ninth century was more like a full-scale invasion than a simple opportunity for plunder.

It was during this prolonged and disastrous incursion of the Norsemen that Edmund, the saintly king of East Anglia, was martyred at their hands. Edmund's forces were overwhelmed by a wave of invaders, and he dismissed his army and tried to flee to Framlingham in Suffolk. He was captured on the way, however, and clapped in irons. At Hoxne, also in Suffolk, the young king was tormented with cudgels and whips, shot full of arrows, and finally beheaded.

Simeon tells us that, having killed two Northumbrian kings in battle at York, the Vikings crowned a puppet king of the region, but eventually the natives forced him out. In response, Halfdan Ragnarsson, a king of the Danes, made his way north. Halfdan was one of the leaders of the so-called Great Heathen Army that caused mayhem in Britain and Ireland at this time. He was also a brother of the intriguingly-named Norse pirates Sigurd Snake-in-the-Eye and Ivar the Boneless; and he may also have been a son of Ragnar Lodbrok (Ragnar of the Hairy Breeches).

The grisly business of conquering, re-conquering and subduing the people of England could not be done so comfortably in the cold part of the year, and so Halfdan decided to spend the winter at Tynemouth. Determined to evacuate his flock before spring, when Halfdan would be on the move again, Bishop Eardulf was unsure whether he should disturb Cuthbert's long sleep and take the saint with him and his brothers. Eardulf consulted with one Eadred, who remembered that Cuthbert had once said that he would rather his bones were moved, than that they should rest in soil controlled by 'schismatics'. 'Schismatics' does not usually refer to pagans (as the Vikings were) and it is possible that Cuthbert had been thinking of Celtic Christians when he used the word. The distinctive Celtic type of Christianity, which had been spread to England by Irish missionaries, had been rejected by the Northumbrians at the Synod of Whitby in 664; after which it seems that Cuthbert, previously a monk in the Celtic tradition, had switched to the Roman strand of Christianity. Eardulf and Eadred decided, however, that Cuthbert's words applied to their situation, and so the saint's body left Lindisfarne with them in the winter of 875.

As it set out on its long wilderness years,

Cuthbert's corpse was joined in its coffin by the head of the saintly King Oswald of Northumbria, and some of the remains of St Aidan. The presence of Oswald's skull in his coffin is the reason why Cuthbert is sometimes depicted holding a king's head. Unfortunately the medieval statue of Cuthbert that now stands by his tomb in Durham cathedral is lacking Cuthbert's own head, though the head of the saintly king is largely intact.

After they left Lindisfarne, there then followed some twelve decades of wandering for Cuthbert and his companions, living and dead. The living community that accompanied the saint's coffin became known as the Haliwork Folk, and, not surprisingly, they seem not to have maintained the strict monastic discipline that had held sway on Lindisfarne. The monks and lay brothers married and had children, and the Haliwork Folk grew organically into a unique, diverse, semi-nomadic community, the nature of which scandalised some clerics who encountered it. When Cuthbert had rested in his present home, the city of Durham, for over eighty years, William de St-Calais, a Norman appointed to the post of bishop of Durham by William the Conqueror, decided to eject these irregular clerical troops and replace them with 'proper' monks. The latter were imported into Durham from the monasteries of Wearmouth and Jarrow.

To return to 875, it seems that Bishop Eardulf's people escaped just in time: Simeon tells us that 'a fearful storm swept over' Lindisfarne and indeed the whole of Northumbria; and the thunderer who brought the metaphorical storm was the ruthless Halfdan. The twelfth-century chronicler Reginald of Durham tells us that the slaughter was so widespread that the native population found themselves on the verge of extinction. Entire cities were set on fire, churches and cemeteries were desecrated, foetuses were cut out of pregnant women, and babies were impaled on spears.

Given the mayhem that was sweeping over England, it is hardly surprising that the custodians of Cuthbert's body should have tried to take their saint out of the country altogether. They attempted to cross to Ireland, but the saint's objection to this plan made itself felt via a terrifying change in the weather.

A terrific storm appeared out of nowhere, and three large waves struck the vessel. Soon it was half-full of water and, strange to say, the sea-water turned to blood. The sailors tried in vain to regain control of the ship, but nothing worked. At last the monks knelt down and begged forgiveness from Cuthbert, for the sin of trying to take their saint away from his own people. At this, the waves grew calm, and a fresh breeze blew the ship back to where it had started, at the mouth of the river Derwent.

One casualty of the sea-storm was a beautifully-made illuminated gospel book, which somehow slid off the ship and fell into the sea. This was the book we now call the Lindisfarne Gospels, made on the island around the beginning of the eighth century, about ninety years before the first Viking raid on Lindisfarne. Thanks to another of Cuthbert's miracles, the gospels, a treasure equal, some would say, to the Dead Sea Scrolls or the death-mask of Tutankhamen, were later discovered unharmed on the beach at Whithorn in south-west Scotland. A man called Hunred or Hundredus, one of the guardians of Cuthbert's body, had been alerted to the location of the lost book (which may have been created as a tribute to Cuthbert) in a dream during which the saint appeared to him.

It was thanks to a similar dream, experienced by Eadred, abbot of the Cuthbert community, that a lowly slave called Guthred was raised to the position of king of Northumbria. Under Guthred, a measure of peace was restored to the northern kingdom, and Cuthbert's bones were able to rest at the old Roman town of Chester-le-Street. It took the saint over a hundred years to travel the few miles south to his final resting place, Durham.

Again, the move was prompted by a dream or 'revelation from heaven', this time granted to Bishop Aldhun of Chester-le-Street. Aldhun's vision instructed him to move Cuthbert's body again, to escape more Viking raids. This time, the body was transported to Ripon, but after a few months it began its journey back to Chester-le-

Street.

At a place called Wurdelau (perhaps Warden Law near Durham) the cart on which Cuthbert's coffin was being carried suddenly became as heavy as a mountain, and could not be moved, though a whole crowd of Cuthbert's people tried to shift it.

It seemed that Cuthbert was trying to tell his guardians that he wanted to stay at Wurdelau, but looking around, anyone could see that the place was uninhabitable. It was a flat, open plain, and offered no natural defences against the inevitable raids from Scots, Vikings and rival Northumbrians for which the local people in those days had to be prepared. Hoping to find a solution to the puzzle their saint had set them, Bishop Aldhun ordered three days of prayer, fasting and 'watching' (meaning going without sleep).

The upshot of all this was that it was revealed to a man called Eadmer that somewhere called Durham should be Cuthbert's final resting-place. This was another puzzle, because none of the Haliwork Folk could remember ever having heard of the place. It was at this point, while the community of St Cuthbert was sitting around scratching its collective head, that a woman appeared, looking for her lost cow. Yes, she knew where Durham was, and she led Cuthbert and his people to the place.

The centre of Durham consists of a tall, flat-topped rock nearly surrounded by a loop in the river Wear. When the monks arrived with their saint, the place was heavily wooded, and it must have looked a lot like the island of Yniswitrin, or Avalon, where, according to legend, Joseph of Arimathea and his companions had built their church only sixty years or so after the birth of Jesus.

An eighteenth-century relief of a woman with her cow can now be seen high on the north wall of Durham's Norman cathedral. This replaces a similar piece of medieval stone-work, and it commemorates the woman who led Cuthbert's people here. Inside the cathedral, Cuthbert still rests under a stone slab at the east end, while his contemporary Bede, who wrote no less than three biographies of Cuthbert, lies in the Galilee chapel at the west end. The building, which is now part of a UNESCO World Heritage Site, and is one of the most important cathedrals in Europe, is a far cry from the temporary shelter of wattles that housed Cuthbert's coffin shortly after he arrived at Durham.

It is hard to overstate the prestige Cuthbert still enjoys in the north country, though he is little-known elsewhere. Not just churches of many different Christian denominations, but also local schools and streets are named after him. When the Durham Anglican Diocese recently moved its headquarters to a new building at the edge of Durham City, 'Cuthbert House' seemed a natural name for the place. Eider ducks, a species of bird that Cuthbert wanted to see protected, are known as 'Cuddy's Ducks' here, and there is even a Cuddy's Cave cheese, named after a place where the saint's coffin is supposed to have been hidden from the Vikings.

*Saint Edward the Confessor, from*
*BL Royal MS 14 B VI, English, C14th*

## III. Edward the Confessor

Some thirty years before England was invaded by the Normans, Alfred Aetheling, a royal prince and brother of the future saint, King Edward the Confessor, arrived in England, ostensibly to visit his mother. He was met at Sandwich, then the most important Channel port on the English coast, by Godwin, the powerful earl of Wessex.

According to a later poem about Edward, written by a monk of Westminster Abbey, Godwin greeted Alfred warmly, embracing him and declaring, 'Now I am content: my rightful king has come. Oh, I have waited for you so long.' But Godwin was speaking with a forked tongue: he was not loyal to Alfred Aetheling, but to King Harold Harefoot, son of Cnut, the late Danish king of England.

That night Godwin's men seized Alfred and his followers. Some of Alfred's men were killed straight away, others were sold into slavery, some were ham-strung, and others were blinded. It was the last fate, blinding, that was inflicted on Alfred Aetheling. Shortly after this, he died at Ely, and was buried in Ely Cathedral.

Brief though it is, the story of Alfred Aetheling's tragic end reveals an awful lot about England during the life of the man who was to become King Edward (called a 'confessor', as St Cuthbert was, because he was a confessor or promoter of the faith, but did not die a martyr).

Alfred's story shows that the times were cruel, and that powerful men like Godwin could literally get away with murdering the son of an earlier king; in this case the son of Aethelred II, known as Aethelred the Unready.

If we look into Godwin's reason for treating Alfred as he did, we find that, though it is defended on two sides by the sea, England was then liable to be taken over by foreign powers: in this case a series of Danish kings. Godwin was loyal to the Danish dynasty; but the Norman influence on English affairs was already great by this time: Alfred and his brother, the future King Edward, had been sheltered by the dukes of Normandy while England was being run by the Danes, and their mother, known as Emma of Normandy, was a sister of one of those Norman dukes.

The story of Alfred Aetheling also demonstrates that in those days a king of England did not achieve his status merely because he was the oldest surviving legitimate son of the previous king. Alfred's father Aethelred had indeed been succeeded by his son Edmund Ironside, but despite his formidable nick-name and his warlike nature, Edmund was forced to agree a truce with Cnut, the Danish invader. Shortly after Cnut and Edmund had divided England between them, Edmund died, leaving Cnut as king of the whole country. When Cnut himself died in 1035, the aforementioned Harold Harefoot became king, even though he was not Cnut's legitimate son. When Harold, in turn, died in 1042, his half-brother Harthacnut succeeded.

It is thought that, shortly after this, the future king and saint Edward the Confessor may have been ruling England in partnership with his half-brother Harthacnut and their remarkable mother, Emma. Emma was remarkable because she managed to marry, have children by, and be widowed by, two kings: first Aethelred the Unready and then Cnut, known as Cnut the Great.

The reader may already have noticed that all the actors in this tangled drama were related, sometimes in complicated ways. The fact that Emma had children by two kings of England, who also fathered children by other women, just adds to the complexity. The international heritage of the parties involved is also notable. Emma, and therefore her son Edward, had not only French but also Danish blood, and even Godwin, the powerful earl of Wessex, was married to a Danish woman, Gytha Thorkelsdóttir.

Thanks largely to the deaths, by various means, of many of his male relatives, including Harthacnut, Edward, later called the Confessor, managed to become King of England in 1043; even though he was only the seventh son of King Aethelred the Unready. One of the deaths that had paved his way to the throne was that of his brother Alfred Aetheling, with whom we began this strange, eventful history.

As well as showing the brutal way that politics could work in eleventh-century England, the various accounts of Alfred's death also demonstrate that, after nearly a thousand years, it is difficult to know exactly what happened to Alfred, and when, and why, and who was really responsible. Alfred's own motivation in visiting England at that time is also something to be guessed at: was he really just visiting his mother, or was he actually planning to make a bid for the English throne?

To modern readers, Alfred's death, following his blinding, might also seem puzzling. A man blinded in an accident or an assault in the twenty-first century would not expect to die as a result. Did Alfred die of shock and heartbreak soon after his blinding, or did an infection set in, that killed him after some weeks or months at Ely? Did the monks at Ely do their best to keep him alive, or did they understand that Alfred's enemies would be very disappointed if he survived? Was Alfred actually blinded, and then murdered by some other means or, as some think, did the knife that blinded him go too deep and enter his brain?

A modern man who suffers trauma to an eye would expect be taken to a hospital, but Alfred found himself at Ely Abbey, being cared for by the monks there. This points up another characteristic of the period: the way that monks and priests filled roles that these days would not usually fall into the laps of clerics. Many lay people turned to monks and nuns for medical care; and holy men of various kinds were expected to act as administrators, diplomats, poets, secretaries, teachers, politicians, historians, counsellors and even military leaders. Edward the Confessor employed a goldsmith who was also an abbot, and later bishop-elect of London. This man, who had the striking name of Spearhavoc (meaning 'sparrowhawk'), was something of an eleventh-century Renaissance man, who also made statues and other *objets d'art*. King Edward entrusted this crafty individual with gold and jewels, expecting that Spearhavoc would make him an imperial crown, to supplement his ordinary kingly crown. Unfortunately, Spearhavoc absconded with these precious items, and managed to vanish without trace. His ultimate fate is still unknown to history.

Whether or not they had tried their best to help Alfred medically, the clerics of Ely found themselves with a royal corpse to dispose of when the Aetheling died in 1036. It seems that some attempt was made to make the late prince into a saint or at least a martyr, but this came to nothing. A more successful attempt had been made to sanctify the memory of Edward the Confessor's namesake and half-uncle, King Edward the Martyr, who was murdered at Corfe in Dorset in 978. This Edward's grandmother Ælfgifu was also venerated at Shaftsbury, as was his father, King Edgar, at Glastonbury.

Given the strong English tradition of making saints out of dead members of the royal family, the later effort to beatify Edward the Confessor was not unusual. The attempt succeeded in 1161, when Pope Alexander III consented to Edward's canonisation. By this time, the saintly king had lain asleep in Westminster Abbey for nearly a century.

In the decades since his death, versions of Edward's life had been written and re-written, and with each re-telling, there was a tendency to add more and more miracles and other saintly features to the king's biography.

One of the authors who tried to sanctify Edward with his pen was Osbert of Clare, prior of Westminster, who wrote a Life of the king in 1138. Osbert knew that Westminster Abbey would benefit enormously if Edward was made a saint, since saints brought pilgrims (the tourists of medieval times) and also gifts from rich and powerful people who wanted to show their piety, and keep the spirit of the saint on their side. A grateful friend in heaven might, after all, be even more useful than a friend at court.

Osbert and his monks at Westminster had reason to be grateful to Edward, even if he had never been thought of as a saintly person. Edward had, after all, restored their ancient abbey, which had languished in a very poor state for many years before his time.

The canonisation of Edward the Confessor also reflects the ancient need of people to be able to look back on a lost golden age, to imagine that their own age may still retain something of that old magic, and to dream that the future might also be blessed by a ruler who not only brought peace and justice, but could also call on the assistance of the angels.

The French rulers of England in the eleventh and twelfth centuries also wanted Edward to be remembered with respect, as they claimed that it was this king who had promised England to Duke William of Normandy, who invaded the country in 1066, the year of Edward's death, and is now remembered as William the Conqueror.

The reason why it is possible that Edward the Confessor promised England to William is that Edward and his wife Edith remained childless after over twenty years of marriage. Although in those Anglo-Saxon days it was not unusual for candidates other than the king's sons to inherit the English throne, the question of the succession tended to be more of a problem if there were no sons, or if the oldest surviving legitimate son at the king's death was a small child. Edward's failure to produce an heir meant that his immediate successor was his nephew, Harold, who ruled for less than a year until he was killed fighting against the Normans at the Battle of Hastings. William the Conqueror insisted that Edward had promised England to him: this assertion was intended to justify the Norman invasion, and the killing of Harold.

The childlessness of Edward and Edith might have been seen, by devotees of Edward's dynasty, the House of Wessex, as a tragic failure, and one of the factors that brought an end to the time of the Anglo-Saxon kings, who had ruled England on-and-off for nearly two hundred years. To the chroniclers who wanted to turn Edward into a saint, however, his childlessness suggested that both he and his wife remained celibate within marriage, and in fact died virgins.

As well as his supposed celibate marriage, Edward's saintly status was also bolstered by his reputation as a man who was prepared to work with his enemies to maintain peace, rather than follow violent vendettas against them, as some of his warlike ancestors would have done. The fact that the king married Edith, the daughter of Godwin, who may have had a hand in the murder of Edward's brother Alfred, is a case in point. Although the hagiographers recognise that Edward never forgave Godwin, they insist that the king lived in perfect amity with his wife, the daughter of his enemy, treating her as one would a beloved sister. This was certainly not true all of the time, as in 1051, the year during which Godwin was forced to flee the country, Edward sent Edith into what amounted to temporary internal exile.

His supposed celibacy and virtuous behaviour in office were used by later writers to sanctify Edward, and various miracles were ascribed to him for the same reason.

Given that his brother Alfred died shortly after having been brutally blinded, it is touching that some of the miraculous cures claimed for Edward involved curing the blind; although Aelred of Rievaulx, a learned abbot of Northumbria, insisted that it was the king's inward purity that enabled him to do this. According to the version of Edward's life written by Aelred in 1163, the king was able to cure blindness simply by touching blind people; and they could also be cured by washing their eyes with water Edward had used to rinse his hands. A servant of the king, who stole away some of this water without the king's knowledge, used it to cure three blind men who were led around by a fourth man, who only had sight in one eye. Thanks to the king's water, even the blind eye of the man with one good eye was cured. Later, at Edward the Confessor's tomb, another six blind men who travelled around with another one-eyed man were all cured.

Although his ability to restore sight to the blind was remarkable, the most famous cures achieved by Edward involved a disease which later became known as the King's Evil. This was probably something called scrofula, a tubercular infection of the lymph glands, which the king was able to dispel just by touching it, though in the first miracle of this type described by Aelred, Edward wet his hands with holy water before attempting a cure.

The lucky recipient of the first of these cures was a young married woman who had so far borne no children. The twelfth-century chronicler William of Malmesbury suggests that the swellings around the woman's neck were caused by her childlessness. Aelred asserts that her symptoms included sterility, a terrible bodily stench, and swellings like acorns; all of which made her so repulsive to her husband that pregnancy became very unlikely.

The unfortunate woman was told in a dream that she should seek the king's help, and Edward washed the woman's swellings, pressed them with his fingers, and marked them with the sign of the cross. This made them burst open immediately, and the worms that had infested them tumbled out. Soon the woman's swellings were replaced by scars, and she later became a happy mother.

Edward's reputation as a solution to the problem of scrofula survived long after his death.

Shakespeare describes Edward's miraculous cures of the 'Evil' in a scene in his play *Macbeth*. In Act IV scene 3, Malcolm explains to Macduff how:

. . . strangely visited people,
All swoll'n and ulcerous, pitiful to the eye,
The mere despair of surgery, he cures,
Hanging a golden stamp about their necks,
Put on with holy prayers. And, 'tis spoken,
To the succeeding royalty he leaves
The healing benediction.

(lines 151-161)

The idea that 'the healing benediction' was passed down 'to the succeeding royalty' was embraced by a succession of English monarchs, right down to George I, who discontinued the practice. From 1633 to 1732 there was even a ceremony for the 'royal touch' set out in the Book of Common Prayer. Charles II, who was restored to the throne in 1660, was particularly keen on the procedure, and may have touched as many as ninety-two thousand sufferers.

It must be said that patients with scrofula nearly always get over it, even without treatment, whether royal, saintly or medical, so any British monarch who 'touched' for the King's Evil was bound to have a pretty good success rate. Spontaneous cures were, however, unlikely to be as rapid as the miraculous cure performed on the young woman who first came to King Edward with this problem.

As well as celibacy, a virtuous life and the ability to perform miraculous cures, Edward was blessed with the faculty of perceiving things that could not be apprehended by those around him. He had visions of both St Peter, and Jesus himself. He could also prophesy future events, and on one occasion became aware of an event that had taken place some four thousand miles away.

This was Edward's vision of the aforementioned Seven Sleepers of Ephesus, something which lends both international and historical aspects to the story of Edward's miraculous abilities.

The story of the Seven Sleepers appears in several early sources, and there is even a Muslim version, in the Qur'an itself (Sura XVIII).

To give the story in more detail than is supplied in chapter one above, it is said that during the brief reign of the third-century Roman emperor Decius, seven young Christian men were arrested when the emperor, an enthusiastic persecutor of Christians, visited the city of Ephesus (now Selçuk in Turkey). The emperor gave the men a little time to consider whether they wanted to become Christian martyrs, or stay alive by agreeing to sacrifice to the pagan gods. When Decius came back to the city, the seven unrepentant Christians were found asleep in a cave. The emperor ordered the cave to be sealed up, thus burying the Sleepers alive.

But the Sleepers, as their name might suggest, did not die. They just went on sleeping, perhaps for nearly two hundred years, until a land-owner called Adolios had the cave opened, intending to use it as a place to keep cattle. By this time, the Roman Empire had become Christian.

As the workmen prised off the cave's seal, the Sleepers awoke, thinking that they had only slept for one night. When everyone, including the Sleepers, understood what had happened, the Christian emperor Theodosius was sent for, and he spoke to these saintly Rip Van Winkles.

The Seven Sleepers of Ephesus entered the story of Edward the Confessor when he saw a waking vision of them during an Easter banquet. Wrapped up in his vision, he laughed aloud as he saw the Sleepers all turn *onto their left sides*. When some of those who were present, including Harold Godwinson, Edward's immediate successor, had heard what the king had seen, a delegation was sent to Ephesus to ascertain the truth. Sure enough, the Sleepers were found to have turned in their sleeps, which everyone recognised as a bad omen.

While the Sleepers lay on their sinister sides for the next seventy years or more, all hell broke loose across Europe and the Middle East. William of Malmesbury, writing about Edward in his

*Chronicle of the Kings of England*, pointed out that during this time, Arabs and Turks overran Syria and Turkey, there were earthquakes, famines and plagues, and political chaos in the royal courts of Europe, and in Rome, the seat of the papacy. There was also a comet seen over England, which was taken as a warning that there would be unsettling changes in the governments of kingdoms.

Bizarre as it already is, the account of the Seven Sleepers given in some of the lives of King Edward adds two extra layers of strangeness to the original story. The earlier accounts insist that the Sleepers died and were buried all together in their cave after their audience with the Roman emperor. But Edward's story suggests that they were still sleeping, in their cave, above ground, in the eleventh century, and that their sleeping positions had some influence over subsequent events in Europe and further afield.

The prophecy of widespread disaster that Edward extracted from his vision of the Seven Sleepers was by no means his only prophetic episode, or his sole experience of seeing events at a distance. It isn't even the only example of his seeing a vision that caused him to laugh. Another episode of this type happened during Mass one Pentecost, when Edward saw, as though through a spiritual closed-circuit television system, the death by drowning of the king of Denmark.

While watching the violent play of two of the

infant sons of the aforementioned Earl Godwin, King Edward also predicted that they would fight a battle against each other when they were adults. This dire prediction, delivered to his father-in-law, was not the only time something miraculous is supposed to have happened when the two of them were together. On the last day of Godwin's life, the pair were sitting at dinner together, when Edward raised the delicate question of the murder of his brother Alfred. The earl tried to demonstrate that he was innocent of the murder by saying that, if he was guilty, his next morsel of food would choke him. It did choke him, and he quickly died. As the earl lay dead under the table, the king asked Godwin's sons to, 'Take this dog away.' (Other accounts of Godwin's death at Edward's dinner-table suggest that no choking was involved, and that he merely suffered a massive stroke.)

On his death-bed, Edward made a final prophecy, or rather conveyed a prophecy that he had learned about in a dream. This prediction was in the form of a puzzle that could not be solved for over thirty years, when the event it prophesied came to pass. The vision predicted that England would be in dire straits until the top of a tree that had been cut off and placed at a distance of three yokes from its trunk was united with the trunk again. According to Aelred, the prophecy concerned the restoration of the descendants of the Anglo-Saxon King Alfred to the English throne. With the death of Edward, three kings (the 'three yokes') who were not related to Alfred reigned, but when King Henry I married the great-granddaughter of Edmund Ironside, Edward the Confessor's brother, the line was restored.

On the Bayeux Tapestry, Edward the Confessor is shown on his death-bed, and also being conveyed after his death to Westminster Abbey, which he had restored at great expense. At the very beginning of the Tapestry, he is shown alive and well and on his throne, wearing a crown. In other depictions, he is shown in similar royal regalia, but holding a ring. This is supposed to be the gold ring that he gave to Saint John the Evangelist, who was disguised as a beggar at the time. This ring was eventually returned to Edward in such a way that he came to know to whom he had given it.

Although the royal tradition of touching for the King's Evil died out in the eighteenth century, the memory of Edward the Confessor is still part of the mystique surrounding the British monarchy; and his remains still lie near the heart of British political power, in Westminster Abbey. It is there that British monarchs are nearly always crowned, and it is thought that up to the time of the Interregnum, when England briefly became a republic, the Confessor's own staff and crown were used in coronation ceremonies. These were destroyed at the Interregnum, but the copies that are now used are still called St Edward's crown and staff. Likewise, the coronation throne, which used to incorporate the Stone of Scone, the

Scottish coronation stone, is called St Edward's chair. This wooden throne is far more ancient than the seventeenth-century staff and crown: it was made in the thirteenth century, and may once have had a picture of Edward, no doubt holding his famous ring, on its back.

*The martyrdom of Thomas Becket, from BL Harley MS 5102, English, C13th*

## IV. Thomas Becket

Edward the Confessor was not canonised until nearly a century after his death, when Pope Alexander III declared him a saint in 1161. In 1159, Alexander had succeeded Pope Adrian IV, a half-forgotten pontiff who is of special interest to English readers, as he was the only Englishman ever elected to the chair of St Peter.

Whether or not Edward deserved to be made into a saint, his canonisation was part of a political deal between the new pope and Henry II, who was king of England at the time. Unfortunately, the papal election following the death of the Englishman Nicholas Breakspear (who had taken the name Adrian IV after his election) managed to choose not one but two popes. These were Victor IV, who had the backing of the powerful red-bearded German emperor, Frederick Barbarossa, and the aforementioned Alexander III.

Some chroniclers say that Victor, the so-called 'antipope', had the backing not only of Barbarossa but of all the monarchs of Europe, except for those of Portugal, Sicily, Spain and Hungary. King

Henry II's backing was therefore crucial, and Pope Alexander expressed his gratitude to the English by allowing one of their old kings to become a saint.

King Henry II had not only pious and patriotic reasons, but also dynastic and political ones, for promoting the canonisation of the Confessor. Henry was related to Edward through his great-grandmother Margaret of Scotland, and the presence of a newly-minted saint on his family tree would, he knew, add greatly to his own prestige.

Aelred of Rievaulx's life of Edward was written to mark the Confessor's canonisation; and a splendid ceremony was held at Westminster Abbey, where the body of the new saint was 'translated' from its grave below ground to a higher position within the shrine that was supposed to have been made for him by William the Conqueror.

The archbishop of Canterbury who attended the translation service, together with a glittering collection of nobles and clerics, was Thomas Becket. In his Life of Becket, the archbishop's friend and counsellor Herbert of Bosham remarked that the ceremony at the abbey was a pleasing demonstration of harmony between King Henry II and Thomas. Herbert adds, however, that this harmony was short-lived.

Although he was related to Edward the Confessor, King Henry II was an altogether different sort of man. He was impatient, and could fly into terrible rages. One spectacular tantrum was provoked by someone praising the king of Scotland in Henry's presence. In response, the king of England screamed, fell out of bed, started tearing up his bed-clothes, and ended up stuffing some of his mattress into his mouth.

The mild-mannered Confessor seems not to have been a avaricious man, and there is even a story to the effect that he forgave a boy whom he caught stealing treasure from his bedroom. Henry II, by contrast, was greedy for land, money and power. He hoped to gain land by fighting wars, particularly in France. He tried to obtain more money by making changes, beneficial to him, to the English tax system of the time; and the additional power that did not come to him through land and money, he hoped to be able to wrestle out of the hands of the Church.

Henry became king after the chaotic reign of King Stephen. Stephen had sat on the throne during the period called the 'Anarchy'. Political chaos was widespread in England at this time because Stephen's claim to the throne was disputed by his cousin, the empress Matilda, daughter of Henry II's grandfather, Henry I. It seems that while civil war raged in England, the Church filled some of the power-vacuum: Henry II was determined to restore royal power to the level he thought had been enjoyed by his grandfather, Henry I.

While Henry II aspired to the level of power he claimed was enjoyed by Henry I, his archbishop of Canterbury, Thomas Becket, looked back to the same period to find inspiration in the life of his predecessor, St Anselm, who was also an archbishop of Canterbury. It is thought that, while Henry II was pressing for the canonisation of Edward the Confessor, Becket succeeded in having Anselm canonised around the same time, and by the same pope.

Part of Henry's strategy to acquire more power was to appoint men loyal to himself to key positions in the government; and in those days this included key positions in the Church.

Although Thomas Becket came from a London merchant family, had not distinguished himself as a great scholar, already held the important position of royal chancellor, and was not even an ordained priest, King Henry secured his appointment as archbishop of Canterbury in 1162, when Thomas was perhaps forty-two years old, and the king not yet thirty. The new archbishop had been ordained only the day before his consecration as archbishop. His predecessor had been his old friend and patron, Theobald of Bec.

The rift with the king probably began shortly after Thomas's consecration when, in a surprise move, the new archbishop resigned his position as royal chancellor. Things escalated at the Council of Westminster, which Henry probably intended to follow on from the ceremony of the translation of Edward the Confessor's remains. Although Herbert of Bosham implies that Becket was central to the canonisation of the Confessor and the translation of his remains, John Guy, in his 2012 book on Thomas, suggests that the archbishop was deliberately sidelined at this event, where the priest in charge was not Becket, but the abbot of Westminster.

Becket was, however, able to claim a relic of Edward the Confessor as the fee for his attendance. Thomas chose a stone section of the tomb of the Confessor, which was connected to one of the miracles King Edward performed after his death.

The miracle concerned St Wulfstan, bishop of Worcester, who was the last Anglo-Saxon to retain his bishopric after the Norman invasion. Lanfranc, an Italian who had in effect been appointed as archbishop of Canterbury by William the Conqueror, demanded that Wulfstan surrender his staff of office and stand down as bishop. Wulfstan then proceeded to the tomb of the Confessor, and thrust his staff into the stone, saying that King Edward could have it, since he had given it to Wulfstan in the first place. The staff, like King Arthur's sword Excalibur, could not then be removed except, of course, by Wulfstan himself. The bishop was thus able to retain his bishopric until his death in 1095.

His possession of the miraculous stone may

have fortified Becket's resolve to stand up to the overbearing King Henry II. The two had already clashed over a tax called 'sheriff's aid', which Henry wanted to be paid straight into his own exchequer. In response, Thomas had threatened that if the tax was to be diverted from its original use by the king, then nobody on any of the estates he, Thomas, controlled would pay it.

The matter of so-called 'criminous clerks' had also become a bone of contention between king and archbishop, and this dominated the proceedings at the Council of Westminster in October 1163.

One way in which the king asserted his power over the kingdom was through the legal system, which he ultimately controlled. It is still the case in England today that the monarch has a great deal of symbolic power over the law: criminal cases are identified by names such as 'The Crown v. Douglas Smith', Smith in this case being the accused.

In twelfth century England, Henry's power over legal proceedings was compromised by a parallel legal system which dealt with crimes committed by clerks; i.e., priests, and others in holy orders. There was a concern that the ecclesiastical courts were handing out more lenient sentences than the secular courts, which tried lay people.

Henry's attention had been drawn to some

cases where 'criminous clerks' had been treated very gently by, for instance, courts presided over by local bishops. There was the case of a clerk from Worcester who is supposed to have seduced the daughter of a local dignitary, then murdered the girl's father. King Henry demanded that this felon be handed over to a secular court, but Becket insisted that he should remain in the custody of the local bishop.

At the Council of Westminster, Henry tried to get the bishops' agreement to the principle that clerks who had committed serious crimes should be stripped of their clerical status by the church courts, so that they could then be handed over to the secular courts, and tried as lay people. This, he implied, would be a return to the way things had been done under his grandfather, King Henry I. He asked the bishops if they would agree to observe this, and other traditional customs. All but one of them, when questioned one by one, said that they would observe these customs, *saving their order*. This meant that they promised to observe them, insofar as it did not contradict their status as churchmen. The one bishop who said something different was Hilary, Bishop of Chichester, who agreed to observe the customs *in good faith*.

To Henry, the majority position of the bishops at the Council of Westminster must have sounded like a group of foxes promising to keep out of the hen-house, unless they felt hungry. Unable to get any further with them, the king, who had, in any case, been in a bad mood all day, swept out, thus bringing the council to an abrupt close. A sequence of events at Westminster that had started with the translation of the newly-canonised Edward the Confessor, a joyful ceremony that showed harmony between the king and the prelates, ended acrimoniously, with the implied threat of further action from the angry king.

The Council of Westminster set the pattern for a series of future meetings between the king, archbishop Thomas Becket, and their representatives, that took place in England and elsewhere, over the next seven years. The two men, who had once been close friends, repeatedly failed to agree, or even compromise satisfactorily. Becket in particular seemed determined to be the opposite of diplomatic; insisting on his rights and those of the Church. Henry must have joined many others close to them both in reflecting that Becket had changed a great deal since he had been a rather worldly royal chancellor, delighting in spectacle and extravagance. Many historians suggest that Thomas underwent some kind of inner conversion, or spiritual re-birth, around the time that he was ordained a priest and enthroned as the archbishop of Canterbury.

During a later council, at Clarendon Palace in Wiltshire, the king again raised the question of the customs that had been observed during his grandfather's day, and which he now wanted to revive. He brought out these customs, written up into a famous document now known as the Constitutions of Clarendon. After prolonged argument, bullying and threats, Becket was prevailed upon to swear to the Constitutions, which were designed to limit the power of the English Church, and increase the power of the king. This was quickly seen by Becket himself as a humiliating climb-down; a cowardly failure.

At this point, Henry might have decided that he had beaten Thomas, and left him alone. But his old friend had now become a thorn in the king's side, and Henry was determined to pluck him out.

At a council at Northampton in October 1164, Henry attempted a legal attack on the archbishop, based on accusations that Becket had acted illegally against one John Marshal, and had embezzled money when he was royal chancellor. Convinced that, whether he was guilty or not, the king had no right to bring such charges against him, Becket made a spectacular exit from the hall, the doors of which seemed to open for him miraculously, of their own accord. Unfortunately the effect of this *coup de théâtre* was slightly spoiled when Thomas nearly fell over a bundle of sticks on his way out.

It was now time for Becket to escape. He slipped out of Northampton castle before dawn, in the pouring rain, and rode hard for Lincoln, attended by only three companions. With the archbishop now in disguise as 'Brother Derman', the fugitives later escaped to France in a humble fishing-boat, departing from Sandwich, where the ill-fated Alfred Aetheling had landed nearly a hundred and thirty years before.

By leaving the country without the king's permission, Becket had gone against clause four of the Constitutions of Clarendon, which he had sworn to, much to his regret, earlier that same year. Once in France, he proceeded to break clause eight of the Constitutions, which forbade English churchmen from appealing to the pope on any matter, without the king's permission. Luckily for Becket, the pope himself was not far away. Kept out of Italy by the power of the German emperor Frederick Barbarossa, Alexander III was in the French city of Sens. Louis VII, the king of France, was even closer, at Soissons.

At Sens, Thomas tried to surrender his archbishopric to Pope Alexander, but after some discussion the pontiff insisted that Becket remain as archbishop of Canterbury. The two men discussed Becket's predicament, and the Constitutions of Clarendon – a discussion which put the pope in an impossible position. He needed the support of kings like Henry II in order to bolster his own weak position as a pope who was unable to take up residence in Rome, and who also had a rival pope to contend with. Although the chronicler Alan of Tewkesbury reports that, when the Constitutions were read out, the assembled bishops and other churchmen at Sens burst into tears, Alexander himself failed to condemn the Constitutions outright.

According to Alan, Alexander then commanded Thomas to go and live in the nearby monastery of Pontigny. Other writers suggest that Thomas himself chose this retreat.

The dispute between Becket and Henry can be characterised as a close friendship that had gone sour, but it also concerned some serious issues that beset Christianity in Western Europe at this time.

Countries like England were, in theory, ruled by hereditary monarchs, but, as we have seen, the power of kings like Henry II was limited by the existence of a semi-separate jurisdiction within their own countries: the power of the pope and his subordinates; the archbishops, bishops and ecclesiastics in the lower ranks, right down to the humble village priests.

The idea of allegiance was very important to medieval people, but to whom did an archbishop, for instance, owe allegiance? If he had sworn to be loyal to God, the pope and the king, then in times of conflict, when the chips were down, did he owe more allegiance to the pope, or the king? Surely, his ultimate allegiance was to God, and the pope was God's representative on earth; but the Christian coronation ceremony, and the existence of royal saints such as Edward the Confessor, meant that the monarch was also, or could be, God's representative as well.

Something like the ugly compound word 'semi-separate' has to be used here because, although in theory the Church should have been free of interference from the secular authorities, in fact the king and his nobles had a great deal of influence over goings-on in their own national church. While Henry II was determined to fasten these powers down with tactics such as his introduction of the written Constitutions of Clarendon, churchmen like Thomas Becket were trying to assert the independent power, income and loyalties of the Church. Meanwhile all of these issues were complicated by the fact that there were both saints and sinners in high office in the Church: while some churchmen inspired love, respect and loyalty, others were known to be greedy and corrupt. In fact Henry had practically opened the Council of Westminster in 1163 by complaining about 'unruly archdeacons' who used their powers as ecclesiastical judges to extort money from sinners – money which they used to finance lives of luxury. The fact that such wicked prelates certainly existed could hardly be disputed at the time, but Henry was using the example of corrupt and even violent and murderous clerics to attack the principle of a separate ecclesiastical system of law.

All these issues, including in particular the nature of the authority of the pope, came under even closer scrutiny at the time of the Reformation, when concerns about the direction in which the Christianity of Western Europe was going led to nothing less than a religious revolution.

The two parallel systems of Church and State, symbolised at the time by the image of the two swords, could coexist peacefully in an atmosphere of compromise, such as seems to have prevailed during the 'golden age' of King Edward the Confessor. But neither Henry nor Thomas seemed to be willing to give an inch in the way of compromise. Becket's stay at Pontigny saw him restraining his pronouncements, mainly because Pope Alexander had insisted on a truce between the English king and his archbishop. But by the time Alexander returned to Rome in 1166, and was no doubt feeling more confident and independent, the truce had expired, and the pope granted Becket the status of a papal legate to England. This meant that the archbishop had the right to excommunicate his enemies with the full authority of the pope. At last, the gloves were back off.

It may be that Henry's production of the written Constitutions at Clarendon had been a surprise to some if not all of the churchmen present at that fraught council. At Vézelay on Whit Sunday 1166, Thomas Becket showed that he, too, could pull rabbits out of hats. In a letter, John of Salisbury, an author who not only knew Thomas Becket as a friend, but had also known Adrian IV, the English pope, described how Becket used his new powers as a papal legate to excommunicate several of those who had acted against him. These included Richard de Lucy, the chief justiciar of England, one of Henry II's most powerful supporters, who practically ran England when Henry was abroad, as he often was. Some claimed that de Lucy had had a hand in writing the Constitutions of Clarendon.

At Vézelay, Becket also threatened to excommunicate the king himself, if he did not show remorse for his actions. John of Salisbury confided to his correspondent that he himself, with others, had persuaded Becket to hold back from declaring an outright sentence of excommunication against the king at that time.

Henry, whose power was not just limited to England, but also stretched across large areas of France, responded to Becket's excommunications by bringing pressure to bear to have Thomas and his followers kicked out of Pontigny: they soon moved to an abbey just outside the walls of Sens.

Although he held so many of the best political cards, and though it must have made him very uncomfortable to do so, Henry did offer a series of compromises in 1169. But Becket regarded these as bait to lure him back to England, and he made the situation worse by announcing another ten excommunications on Palm Sunday in that same year.

The long stalemate was broken in June 1170, when Henry weakened his position vis-à-vis the

Church by having his fifteen year-old son crowned king in Westminster Abbey. This strange business of crowning the king's son before his royal father's death was a revival of an old French custom: after this, the son was known as 'Henry the Young King' to distinguish him from his father.

The coronation was outrageous to both Becket and the pope because the archbishop of York had conducted the ceremony, when by right Thomas Becket, as archbishop of Canterbury, should have been in charge. Becket was now determined to return to England to sort out the mess, and to punish the churchmen who had acted against him both at the coronation and at other times. A substantial peace was at last agreed at an emotional meeting between Becket and Henry near Fréteval in the French province of Touraine, and following some delay, the archbishop was ready to return to England after an exile of seven years.

Standing on the Channel coast at Wissant, north of Boulogne, Becket was approached by one Milo, the dean of Boulogne, who conveyed a message from Matthew, the count of Boulogne.

'Beware,' he said. 'There are people waiting, ready to murder you. The ports are blockaded: when you take to sea, they are ready to seize your ship and butcher everyone on board; or put you all in chains.'

'Brother,' Thomas replied, 'even if my body were torn to pieces, I could not deviate from the path I am now on. Nothing can call me back – not even the threat of danger or torture. My flock has been without me for seven years: that is long enough. I have already made my last request to all my men (and they must obey this, because it is my last wish). I have begged them to carry my dead body into the church that I have deserted for so long, if the Lord decides that I should be killed before I get there.'

Having arrived at Sandwich, Becket was greeted enthusiastically by the common people, but it became clear that many from the ruling class still held a grudge against him. These included the bishops and others who had been excommunicated by him for their participation in the crowning of the Young King. One of Becket's most prominent enemies among the laity was Ranulf de Broc, who had been given the archbishop's lands to administer while the archbishop himself was in exile. Becket accused de Broc of administering his lands badly, and, in effect, of profiteering. The archbishop managed to excommunicate de Broc three times.

When Becket was forced to flee to Canterbury, the de Brocs, according to the chronicler William Fitzstephen, prepared night-time ambushes for him and his followers, so that he could not escape. Ranulf de Broc later aided and abetted, and probably led, the men who murdered Thomas Becket, though he struck no blows himself.

The de Broc family had a vested interest in seeing Becket's fall, but they were not such dangerous enemies as the hot temper of King Henry II, which is what ultimately led to the archbishop's death.

Henry was at a place called Bur-le-Roi in Normandy when he received a letter from two bishops and an archbishop: Roger de Pont L'Évêque, archbishop of York, Jocelin de Bohun, bishop of Salisbury, and Gilbert Foliot, the bishop of London. According to the French verse life of Becket by Garnier of Point-Sainte-Maxence, the letter was the official notice these churchmen had been sent by the pope, informing them of their excommunications. This so infuriated the king that he clapped his hands together and went white with rage. It is at this point in the story that, according to popular legend, he is supposed to have said something like, 'Will no one rid me of this troublesome priest;' but according to Garnier, Henry was guilty of a much longer rant, which ended with him expressing his anger and amazement that nobody had avenged him.

The king's apparent desire for revenge is supposed to have set off a conspiracy, headed by four barons who quickly left Bur-le-Roi and made their way to England, where they were assisted by the aforementioned Ranulf de Broc. The barons, who are usually referred to as 'the knights', were Reginald FitzUrse, Hugh de Morville, William de Tracy and Richard le Bret.

The conspirators took control of enough local castles, and gathered enough men, to resist a force of Becket's supporters, if they should rise up against them. They even had enough man-power to lay siege to Canterbury if necessary. But in his last minutes, when the Canterbury monks tried to bar the doors of the cathedral against the assassins, Becket insisted that the house of God should never be a fortress, and that the doors should be left unbarred.

And so the murderous knights entered unimpeded, and began to demand that Becket cancel his excommunications, or die. According to the eye-witness account of Edward Grim, who nearly lost an arm when he tried to protect the archbishop, the first blow was struck by Reginald FitzUrse, who cut off the top of Becket's head. De Tracy and le Bret also struck the archbishop, and at last his body fell to the floor. De Morville seems to have occupied himself fighting off anyone who tried to come to the archbishop's assistance. At last one Hugh Mauclerk, who had accompanied the killers, put his foot on Becket's neck, and scattered his brains across the floor. As they all left, Meauclerk remarked that their victim would not be getting up again.

Thomas Becket's murder immediately put King Henry in the wrong: the question of whether he was directly responsible for it was largely irrelevant. Overnight, it seems, the controversial archbishop started to be regarded as a saint, and

Henry was cast in the role of Pilate, or Herod, or one of the persecuting Roman emperors.

Becket's posthumous miracles started before his blood was dry on the floor of his cathedral. William Fitzstephen, another witness of the murder, relates how a local man who had been in the cathedral when the archbishop was killed dipped the edge of his shirt in the martyr's blood and returned to his home in the city. There he mixed the blood with some water, and the resulting mixture was used to wash his wife, who had been suffering from paralysis for some time. She was cured on the spot. Soon tin ampoules containing a mixture of water and saintly blood were being distributed to pilgrims, and miraculous cures were effected. Some of the beneficiaries, Fitzstephen tells us, were even raised from the dead.

*From the frontispiece of William Roper's biography of Thomas More, 1626*

## V. Thomas More

Thomas Becket and Thomas More had more in common than just their first names. Both were close friends and servants of English kings (who were both called Henry) and both were martyred because of the attitude of kings who turned against them. Both lived during periods when politics and religion were really inseparable; both stood up for rights and principles that frustrated the desires of their monarchs, and both, by their deaths, assumed much greater and more lasting significance than they ever had in life.

Both More and Becket were also the heroes of magnificent British films made in the mid-1960s, based on plays written in the 1950s. Unfortunately *Becket* (1964), starring Richard Burton in the title role, has not achieved the lasting success enjoyed by the 1966 film *A Man For All Seasons*, starring Paul Schofield as Thomas More.

Superb though it is, the film of *Becket*, based on a play by the French dramatist Jean Anouilh, reflects Anouilh's belief that Becket himself was a

Saxon, liable to be looked down on by the French hierarchy that ruled England at the time. This is almost certainly not true: both of Becket's parents were probably Normans.

Thomas More shared a first name with Canterbury's chief saint, but he also shared the name 'Thomas' with three other Thomases who, like More, were close advisers to King Henry. These were Thomas Cranmer, Thomas Wolsey and Thomas Cromwell. It shows the character of King Henry that of these four Thomases only one outlived the much-married king: two of them were executed, and one, though he was never led to the block, still died as a result of Henry's actions against him. This was Thomas Wolsey, who died a broken man at Leicester while making a desperate attempt to return to London to answer a charge of treason. Although Cranmer outlived King Henry, he still managed to be burned at the stake under Henry's daughter, Mary.

Both Thomas More and Thomas Becket were born in London, and although they both achieved great prominence, More as lord chancellor and Becket as both royal chancellor and archbishop of Canterbury, neither of them came from aristocratic families. Both More and Becket also gave up their roles as chancellors, against the wishes of their respective Henries.

Both Thomases had also benefited, as youngsters, from the patronage of archbishops of

Canterbury: Becket lived in the household of Archbishop Theobald of Bec, More in the house of Archbishop John Morton.

But who was this Thomas More, who followed so closely in the footsteps of his earlier namesake? The question is best answered by beginning with one of the many celebrated stories about him.

Walking by the Thames one day, Thomas More remarked that he would willingly be tied up in a sack and thrown into the river, 'upon condition that three things were well established in Christendom'.

More's companion naturally asked him what these three things were. Thomas replied:

> The first is, that where the most part of Christian princes be at mortal war, they were all at an universal peace. The second, that where the Church of Christ is at this present sore afflicted with many errors and heresies, it were settled in a perfect uniformity of religion. The third, that where the king's matter of his marriage is now come in question, it were to the glory of God and quietness of all parties brought to a good conclusion.

More's desire for world peace, even among Christians, would still be unsatisfied if he were alive today, as would his longing for uniformity of religion. His third concern, 'the king's matter of his marriage' was settled during More's own life, but whether it was settled 'to the glory of God and quietness of all parties' is something that has been debated by historians for nearly five hundred years.

The king in question here is of course Henry VIII, who was crowned in 1509. The 'matter of his marriage' did not become an issue until the 1520s, when he seems to have started to panic about his wife's failure to produce a male heir.

Henry's first marriage, to the Spanish princess Katherine of Aragon, which was celebrated just weeks after his coronation, could only happen because of a special dispensation from the pope, because Katherine had previously been married to Henry's older brother Arthur, who died in 1509. Henry seems to have become obsessed by the idea that this marriage was against both divine and natural law, and that the couple's failure to produce a male heir who could survive beyond infancy was a punishment from God for their 'incest'.

The story is one of the best-known in English history, and has featured in many factual or 'fictionalised' historical books, in films, and TV dramas and documentaries. As a subject, Henry VIII's first divorce and second marriage was even tackled by Shakespeare in his late play *The Famous History of the Life of King Henry VIII*, which he wrote in collaboration with his fellow-playwright, John Fletcher. Shakespeare is also thought to have contributed to an earlier play, *Sir Thomas More.*

Henry's desire to be divorced from Katherine, or to have his marriage annulled on the grounds of incest, was sharpened when he became infatuated with the dark, slender young Anne Boleyn; and over the next seven years or so he grew increasingly impatient with the pope's refusal to grant him a divorce or an annulment.

The upshot was that Henry cut his country off from Rome by passing a series of laws that must have seemed like a succession of violent legal earthquakes to English people who wanted their country to remain part of the European Roman Catholic family. At last, Henry married Anne in 1533, and she was crowned queen in the same year. In the next year, the Act of Supremacy came into force, replacing the pope as head of the English church with King Henry and his successors. This Act is still in force, and the reigning British monarch remains the head of the Church of England to this day.

The Treasons Act, passed in the same year, made it treason to object to the Act of Supremacy, and Thomas More, who had been Henry's lord chancellor, was executed under this Act because he refused to swear to the Act of Supremacy.

We know about Thomas More's wish to be tied up in a bag and thrown into the Thames because his companion on his riverside walk, his son-in-law William Roper, wrote an important biography of his father-in-law during the brief reign of the Roman Catholic Queen Mary. Perhaps because this biography tended to make a hero of a man who had been declared a traitor, it was not actually published until 1626.

Many of us might idly say that we would be happy to die if only certain problems in the world could be settled; but self-sacrifice, self-denial and a monkish humility seem to have been hard-wired into the personality of Thomas More; a man who was really remarkable in many respects. The term 'a man for all seasons' was used by the grammarian Robert Whittington in his *Vulgaria*, published in 1520:

> More is a man of an angel's wit and singular learning. I know not his fellow. For where is the man of that gentleness, lowliness and affability? And, as time requireth, a man of marvellous mirth and pastimes, and sometime of as sad gravity. A man for all seasons.

In the sixteenth century, the word 'sad' meant something more like our modern word 'serious', but Whittington's compliment captures the mixture of gravity and light-heartedness that made More so attractive to many of his contemporaries, and has continued to recruit new admirers for him right into the twenty-first century.

In modern times, More has become an archetype of the individual who sacrifices everything because of a conscientious objection.

As well as sacrifice, self-denial and humility, personal integrity and deep religious faith motivated More. We learn from William Roper that as a young man in London More 'gave himself to devotion and prayer in the Charterhouse of London, religiously living there, without vow, about four years'. This probably means that he lived with London's Carthusian monks, and that he may have entertained the idea of becoming one of them, although his glittering career as a lawyer was already under way by this time.

Even when More abandoned any ideas he may have had of embracing the life of a monk, and began to think of marriage, he showed remarkable self-denial. By then he was living in the house of 'one Master Colt, a gentleman of Essex', where he took a shine to Colt's second daughter; 'but of a certain pity framed his fancy towards' the first daughter, because of the 'great grief and some shame' she might feel if her younger sister were married before her.

As More's eminence in the London legal world grew, he established an estate for himself and his family at Chelsea, where, it is widely reported, the Mores all lived together happily, virtuously and productively. More wrote his famous political fantasy *Utopia* in 1516, and it seems that he was trying to create the ideal utopian Christian household in his fine house in what was then a village near Westminster. One of the admirable features of More's approach to bringing up his own children was his insistence that the girls should be educated to a high standard. Margaret, the daughter who married William Roper, was remarkably well-educated for a woman of her time, and even published a translation of a Latin work by More's friend, the Dutch humanist Erasmus of Rotterdam.

More's affection for his home and family may have been one reason why he was at first reluctant to enter the king's service, and as Henry VIII grew closer to his brilliant lawyer friend, Thomas's precious time at home was cruelly curtailed. Even when they had no business to discuss, Henry would summon More, who could be very amusing company, to the palace 'to be merry' with the king and queen at supper. This became such a problem for the home-loving More that he decided to rein in his winning humour and, in Roper's words, 'somewhat to dissemble his nature, and so by little and little from his former accustomed mirth to disuse himself, that he was of them from thenceforth at such seasons no more so ordinarily sent for'.

The picture of Thomas, Henry and Queen Katherine making merry over supper when the day's business had been concluded is an attractive one, but in hindsight, it is tinged with bitterness. Later Henry would have Thomas killed, and he would also move heaven and earth to cast off his first queen and marry his mistress. Worse, he attempted to disinherit Mary, his daughter by

Katherine, and make any children of Anne Boleyn his heirs.

At the height of their friendship, King Henry would visit More's mansion in Chelsea, and walk around the garden with his arm around More's shoulders. This was a sign of favour that the king bestowed only on his best-loved servants, but it does not evoke an entirely positive picture. Henry was a tall, strongly-built man, which More certainly was not. More's shoulder might have fitted right under Henry's arm-pit, and the weight of that brawny, Tudor arm, which could not be shaken off without giving grave offence, must surely have seemed oppressive at times.

When his son-in-law William Roper complimented More on the favour the king was showing him, Thomas replied with an observation that revealed his own sense of the precariousness of his position, and perhaps his insight into the true character of the outwardly amiable Henry. 'I thank our Lord, son,' said More, 'I find his Grace my very good lord indeed, and I believe he doth as singularly favour me as any subject within this Realm. Howbeit, son Roper, I may tell thee I have no cause to be proud thereof, for if my head could win him a castle in France it should not fail to go.'

More's words here are ambiguous: did he mean that Henry would surely decapitate him if there was a chance of gaining a French castle by the act; or did he mean that he, Thomas More, would gladly *give* his head to win the king such a castle? It hardly matters: in either case, here More reveals his awareness that, as the duke of Norfolk once reminded him, *the wrath of a prince is death*.

At the height of his career as a government official, More became lord chancellor, but he seems to have gone out of his way to make his time basking in the sun of King Henry's favour less luxurious than it could have been. He kept to his modest way of life, avoided bribes and what we would now call 'sweeteners', interpreted the laws impartially, ate and drank plainly and sparingly, devoted time to prayer and study, and even wore a hair shirt next to his skin, as Thomas Becket had done. For a long time, only his favourite daughter, the aforementioned Margaret, knew about the hair shirt: it was her duty to wash it.

As well as being merry with the king, More used his superior education, penetrating intelligence, and skill as a writer, to aid Henry in his intellectual pursuits. Remembered now as a paranoid, grotesque monster, there had been much optimism about Henry VIII when he first ascended the throne, because of his educational accomplishments. Together with Bishop John Fisher, who was martyred in the same year as Thomas More, More helped the king put together his treatise *The Defence of the Seven Sacraments*, an influential attempt to strike a blow in favour of the Roman Catholic Church and the supremacy of the pope, written to counter the doctrines then being promulgated by the German Protestant reformer, Martin Luther.

One of the accusations later levelled against More was that 'by his subtle sinister slights' he had 'most unnaturally' provoked the king into writing this book which, when Henry turned against the papacy, only served to 'put a sword into the pope's hands'. This charge was put to More at a tense meeting with the archbishop of Canterbury, the lord chancellor, the duke of Norfolk and Thomas Cromwell. In response, More reported that, when he was helping the king with the composition of his treatise, he had advised him not to assert the authority of the pope so strongly. 'Nay,' said the king, '. . . we are so much bounden unto the See of Rome that we cannot do too much honour unto it.'

King Henry's *Defence of the Seven Sacraments* was part of the long drawn-out war of words between Luther and his followers one one side, and those who remained loyal to the Roman Catholic religion on the other. The *Defence* was answered by Luther in his book *Against Henry, King of the English*, and this was in turn contradicted by More's *Responsio ad Lutheram*. Henry was given the title Defender of the Faith by Pope Leo X as a reward for writing his *Defence*, and the king told More that it was from the pope that he had received the right to wear an imperial crown, like the one Edward the Confessor had tried to have made for himself centuries earlier. But as 'the king's matter of his marriage' rumbled on, Henry was prepared to cut off the pope who had honoured him, listen attentively to well-worn objections to the Roman faith, and embrace some of the ideas of his old intellectual sparring-partner, Martin Luther.

Henry had wanted More looking over his shoulder as he wrote his *Defence*, and according to William Roper, the king also insisted on consulting with Thomas very shortly after Cardinal Wolsey had persuaded the bishop of Lincoln 'to put a scruple into His Grace's head, that it was not lawful for him to marry his brother's wife'. The king wanted More's agreement on this matter, but he never got it, and as the years passed, the king's disappointment turned to murderous rage.

When Henry first raised the matter with More, Thomas pleaded that this was a matter of divinity (what we might now call theology) and that as such he was not qualified to comment on it. But the king pressed him, and More begged for time to go off and study the issues. At last, he reported that, though the bishops of Bath, and Durham, might have approved of the king's re-marrying; 'St Jerome, St Augustine and divers other old Holy Doctors, both Greeks and Latins' did not.

Later, at his trial at Westminster Hall, More again relied on what he understood to be the opinions of those who were 'now holy saints in heaven,' asserting that 'I am very sure it is the far greater part of them that, all the while they lived, thought in this case that way that I think now. And therefore am I not bound . . . to conform my conscience to the council of one realm against the general council of Christendom'.

More had been brought from his imprisonment in the ill-omened Tower of London to answer his enemies' accusations at Westminster Hall, and it is his cheerful attitude, both to his imprisonment and to his looming execution, that brought out the true strength of his character.

While Henry, and the rest of England, as it must sometimes have seemed, were prepared to turn their coats, and also to turn their backs on Rome, Thomas More and many in his circle were not. For them, their conscientious objection made conformity impossible, and it would seem that the example of the sufferings of Jesus and his saints, which More often called to mind, were an inspiration and a strength.

More's attitude to his incarceration showed that, like St Cuthbert, the 'man for all seasons', was content with both the solitary and the public life. Whereas Cuthbert thrived on his remote island, but could also do well in the much more public role of a bishop, More was able to live happily in the constant presence of family, friends, clients and colleagues, and also in the enforced solitude of his prison. When Margaret, that favourite daughter, visited him, he told her that:

I believe . . . that they that put me here, ween [think]

> they have done me a high displeasure. But I assure thee . . . if it had not been for my wife, and you that be my children . . . I would not have failed long ere this to have closed myself in as strait [tight] a room and straiter too.

This was More's monkish side re-asserting itself, as it had when he built the so-called New Building near his house at Chelsea, 'wherein there was a chapel, a library and a gallery. In which, as his use was upon other days to occupy himself in prayer and study together'. But as a brilliant author, Thomas also seems to have relished the opportunity that incarceration in the Tower gave him to write, although both William Roper and a slightly later biographer, Nicholas Harpsfield, insist that, as Harpsfield puts it, 'the most part' of these prison writings were 'written with none other pen in the world than with a coal', probably meaning a piece of charcoal.

More's remarkable *Dialogue of Comfort Against Tribulation* was written in the Tower, and its author now sits in very good company with other authors of celebrated prison works: these include St Paul, the Roman philosopher Boethius, Sir Walter Ralegh and Oscar Wilde.

When More implied to his beloved daughter Meg that 'if it had not been for my wife, and you that be my children' he would have taken up something like the life of a hermit long before his time in the Tower, it is clear that he was touching on the thing that made his upcoming self-sacrifice most difficult to contemplate. More is the only one of our five English saints who is known to have had children of his own, and the thought of having to leave them, bereft of his protection, was no doubt a torment of a type which none of our other four saints had to face.

During the prison visit from his daughter Margaret, when he admitted his long-standing wish to live as a hermit, More also said that he trusted that God would help his family, and 'supply my lack among you'. He added, 'I find no cause, I thank God, Meg, to reckon myself in worse case here than in mine own house, for me thinketh God maketh me a wanton, and setteth me upon his lap and dandleth me'.

By this time, More's first wife, Jane Colt, had been dead for twenty-five years. Shortly after Jane's death, More had married a wealthy, older widow, Alice Middleton. While it is clear that his beloved Meg, whose mother was Jane, understood his principled stand, it would seem from Roper's account that Alice did not. Visiting him in the Tower, she complained:

> I marvel that you, that have been always hitherto taken for so wise a man, will now so play the fool to lie here in this close, filthy prison . . . seeing you have at Chelsea a right fair house, your library, your books, your gallery, your garden, your orchard . . . where you might in the company of me your wife, your children

and household be merry . . .

In response More, who by now seems to have been viewing his own life from the point of view of eternity, asked her if their home in Chelsea was any nearer heaven than the Tower.

Whether More obtained immortality in heaven after his execution on Tower Hill on the sixth of July 1535 is something that we, who live below the moon, cannot know. The martyr's many modern Christian admirers would not doubt it; but More has his detractors as well. Chief among these in terms of literary fame was John Foxe (1516-87) who accused More of various crimes in his *Acts and Monuments*, commonly called *Foxe's Book of Martyrs*.

Foxe's charge against More is that, as Lord Chancellor and an enemy to Protestants, whom he thought of as 'heretics', he interrogated people who went on to be burned at the stake. Foxe also claimed that More imprisoned suspects in his own house, set them in his own domestic stocks, flogged them as a punishment or to exact confessions, and, in the case of one John Tewkesbury, had 'small ropes' tightened round his head until 'blood started out of his eyes'.

Foxe made his claims long after More had died; but similar accusations had been levelled at him during his life. In response, he denied ever using corporal punishment, except against Dick

Purser, a servant of his who had uttered what More regarded as heresy; and a madman who had muttered 'frantic heresies' and disrupted church services by lifting up women's skirts. Even Foxe, who had included the John Tewkesbury story in the first edition of his *Acts and Monuments*, withdrew it for the second.

That More, as lord chancellor, and in his other positions of authority, had been complicit in the deaths of 'heretics' is, however, impossible to deny, and recent biographers of the great man have all had to come to terms with this aspect of More's life, whether their underlying attitude to their subject is positive or otherwise. John Guy argues that More's persecuting activities were a practical extension of his work as an opponent of Protestantism: work that started with the assistance he gave King Henry when that monarch was putting together his *Defence of the Sacraments*. Guy also points out that legal action against what the state defined as heretics was part and parcel of More's duties as lord chancellor, and servant to a king who was then determined to uphold the Roman Catholic faith.

As is the case in many modern murder trials, the degree to which we allow tales of floggings and burnings to help us determine More's guilt or otherwise may depend on our assessment of what More was thinking at the time. In an essay in *The Cambridge Companion to Thomas More* (2011) Richard Rex asks us to try to see the matter through More's own eyes; and a strange little passage in William Roper's biography of his father-in-law may offer us the opportunity to do this.

In this passage, Roper recounts how, in a conversation with More, he praised the state of affairs in England, saying that the country was lucky to have 'so Catholic a prince that no heretic durst show his face'.

'And yet, son Roper, I pray God,' said More, 'that some of us, as high as we seem to sit upon the mountains, treading heretics under our feet like ants, live not [to see] the day that we gladly would wish to be at league and composition with them, to let them have their churches quietly to themselves, so that they would be content to let us have ours quietly to ourselves'.

Here More seems to be employing the gift of insight (some might call it prophecy) that he often used, to give Roper a glimpse of a possible future for England, when the Protestants would be in charge, and the Catholics begging them for a little space in which to continue their own religion. That More hoped neither himself nor the others incorporated in his phrase 'some of us' would live long enough to see that day hints at the degree to which he dreaded Protestantism, and saw it as a threat, like a foreign invasion, to be fought off at all costs.

The Catholic dread of Protestantism in power

is amply represented in the aforementioned biography of More by Nicholas Harpsfield. Harpsfield's account makes up a third of his book *Three Thomases,* which he probably wrote in the late 1550s. The other two Thomases were Thomas Becket and Thomas the Apostle, known as Doubting Thomas. In a section where he breaks off from the subject of Thomas More and tries to cast shade on Henry VIII's Act of Supremacy, Harpsfield points up what he clearly saw as the tragic absurdity of England's break with Rome, invoking the name of Lucius, king of the Britons:

> What country then was it of all the provinces of the Roman Empire that first publicly and openly, with their people and their King, received and embraced the Christian faith? Was it not the people of this our Britain with our blessed King Lucius?

Later Harpsfield argues:

> . . . so we were the first that with common consent and public law forsook the unity of the Catholic Church, and gave the Pope's spiritual supremacy to a temporal king. For albeit the Grecians long ago abandoned the See of Rome, and of late the Germans, yet were they never so bad or mad as to attribute the said supremacy to any lay Prince . . .

If he had lived to see the later persecution of Roman Catholics in England, More might have regretted that he hadn't fought even harder against the rise of Protestantism, when he had the opportunity, and England's Church was still anchored to Rome.

Thomas More was beheaded at the Tower of London on the sixth of July, 1535. Seeing that the scaffold was as rickety as the reasons for which he was being executed, he seized a last opportunity to be merry. 'I pray you, master lieutenant,' he said, 'see me safe up, and for my coming down, let me shift for myself.'

# VI. Reflections

It is striking that the five saints who are given most attention in the above chapters all lived through times of great change.

Alban lived at a time when the growth of Christianity was beginning to be seen as such a threat to the existence of the Roman empire that emperors and their agents were prepared to go to great lengths, and perpetrate heart-breaking atrocities on a grand scale, to try to prune back the growth of the new religion.

Cuthbert, whose life overlapped with the lives of St Oswald and St Aidan, lived at a time when Christianity was increasing in importance in the north of England, but when Christian leaders still fought pitched battles against pagans and when, as the incident by the Scottish Tyne demonstrated, many were still unsure about Christ, and his followers who lived among them. Cuthbert was also present at the Council of Whitby in 664, when it was decided that Northumbria, at least, should embrace the Roman form of Christianity, and cast off the Celtic form.

Edward the Confessor died just months before the Norman invasion of England in 1066, and generations of historians have naturally regarded his long reign as a prelude to the massive changes that the arrival of William the Conqueror caused in every part of English society.

Thomas Becket, who thrived and then suffered and died under another English king of French ancestry, saw England aspiring to a continental empire, and challenging secular and ecclesiastical power on an international scale.

Thomas More was close to another King Henry who, like Henry II, resorted to extreme measures to gain complete control, and who suppressed opposition by any means available.

As well as living in times of change, our five saints were all mixed up in politics in one way or another. Apart from Alban, who had to deal with the hierarchy reigned over by the emperor in Rome, all of them dealt directly with English monarchs, and of course Edward the Confessor eventually became a monarch himself.

Although the Christian leaders of their times: popes, archbishops, bishops and missionaries in particular, sometimes seemed to be trying to carve out a separate sphere of influence, the 'separation of powers' that is so cherished in modern secular societies hardly existed for our saints; and the Church could not flourish without the encouragement, or at least the consent, of secular leaders. As the story of the Seven Sleepers of Ephesus demonstrates, the Christianisation of Europe was indeed a remarkable change, but within the context of the Roman empire it could hardly have been achieved or sustained unless the emperors themselves were Christian, or at least tolerant of Christianity.

In the Middle Ages, the overlap between the secular and religious worlds reflected the mind-set of the times, which often seemed unable to consider human beings other than in terms of their relationship to God; and by extension lent certain objects, places, events and people an air of divine significance that amounted to something like enchantment.

The role of the saints as people who connected heaven and earth, and sometimes had insight into the realities of hell, was surely central to many peoples' understanding of the universe: for them, the existence of saints among them, or near them in history, meant that the divine torch was still glowing, and that their God was still active and relevant.

# VII. Notes

## ALBAN

### Hepatomancy

Hepatomancy is the explanation behind some of the oddest artefacts that are sometimes found by archaeologists at Roman sites. These items are models of the livers of various animals, with inscriptions on them to indicate what the hepatomancer should look out for.

### Eating Meat Sacrificed to Idols

The believers who sent their apologies to the disappointed hostess were probably basing their reservations about the meat she was serving on a passage in the Bible. There is a discussion about whether Christians should eat meat from animals sacrificed to idols in the eighth chapter of Paul's first letter to the Corinthians, in the New Testament. The Christians of Diocletian's time may have interpreted this chapter as a prohibition against eating such meat, but the chapter may not apply directly to their dilemma, since in verse ten it becomes clear that Paul is talking about eating *inside a pagan temple.*

## Romula's Dinner-Parties

Galerius's mother's angry feelings about the Christians, which are said to have helped to provoke Diocletian to torture and kill many of them, may seem petty; but it is likely that her dinner-parties were very important to Romula: she probably used them as a way to 'network', in modern terms: to make important political alliances and to firm up the power-bases of her son, herself and her family in general. As a woman, Romula would have had limited access to the official centres of power in the Roman Empire: she may have felt that she needed this back-door, unofficial access to count politically.

## Saint George

The idea that George was both a saint and a soldier made him very attractive to people raised in the barbaric aristocratic culture of medieval Europe, where many boys were brought up to believe that knighthood was the right aspiration to cherish all through childhood and adolescence. The appeal of George to the knights and nobles who 'crusaded' against the superior civilization of Islam may explain why George became England's patron saint. It is just possible that the legend of George and the dragon may have something to do with the writer of some lost text, which identified Diocletian as the wicked dragon who laid waste to the Christian population of his empire.

'Protomartyr Anglorum'

This is actually a misnomer, since there was no place called England in Alban's time, and the Angles, who gave England its name, hadn't yet taken control.

The First Church at Glastonbury

The church is supposed to have been built of 'wattles', which perhaps means that it had the wattle-and-daub construction of many ancient English buildings. If it had been built of wattles alone, it would have been more like the first church built for St Cuthbert at Durham in 995 AD. This would have been little more than a temporary shelter – perhaps a tent of sticks and leaves – and nobody would have expected it to last for over a century.

## CUTHBERT

### Cuthbert's Origins

The fact that the story of the monks on the rafts is set in what we now call Scotland indicates that Cuthbert may originally have come from there.

### Cuthbert's Miracles

As well as resembling the miracles of Jesus and his disciples, some of Cuthbert's miracles as related by Bede stand alone as isolated stories and, as in the case of Edward the Confessor, some of these miracles closely resemble each other. This naturally gives rise to suspicions about the provenance of these miracle-stories. Might they not have become attached to Cuthbert's life retrospectively?

### Cuthbert's Illness

There has long been speculation that the north's

favourite saint suffered from some chronic form of disease, that occasionally flared up and laid him low. In the late nineteenth century a Durham medic called Dr Selby Plummer suggested that various clues in Cuthbert's biography point to this having had tuberculosis, of a type that affected various parts of his body, and not just his lungs. Though today we tend to associate TB with Dr Plummer's own century, it is in fact a very ancient disease. In suffering from a chronic illness, Cuthbert was like St Paul, who described his own mysterious long-term condition as like a thorn in his side.

## EDWARD THE CONFESSOR

### Virginity

The high price some Christians still put on virginity and celibacy is a characteristic of the Christian religion that has remained with it almost from the beginning of Christianity itself. Jesus is supposed to have been born of a virgin, and Jesus himself, and St Paul, the apostle to the Gentiles, are both supposed to have remained unmarried virgins. Monks, nuns and priests in the Roman Catholic tradition are still expected to remain celibate, and many other Christian sects expect their lay followers to stay celibate until marriage. The current Roman Catholic Catechism recommends celibacy within marriage as one way to avoid unwanted pregnancies without using 'unnatural' forms of birth control.

# Select Bibliography

## Alban

Bede: *The Ecclesiastical History of the English People*, Oxford, 1999
Geoffrey of Monmouth: *The History of the Kings of Britain*, Penguin, 1966
Lactantius: *Of the Manner in Which the Persecutors Died* translated by William Fletcher, from *Ante-Nicene Fathers*, Vol. 7, Christian Literature Publishing, 1886
Robinson, J. Armitage: *William of Malmesbury 'On the Antiquity of Glastonbury'* in *Somerset Historical Essays*, British Academy, 1921

## Cuthbert

Bede: *The Ecclesiastical History of the English People*, Oxford, 1999
Simeon of Durham: *A History of the Church of Durham*, Llanerch, 1993

Webb, J.F. (ed.): *The Age of Bede*, Penguin, 1998

Edward the Confessor

Aelred of Rievaulx: *The Historical Works*, Liturgical Press, 2008
Barlow, Frank: *Edward the Confessor*, Yale, 1997
Carpenter, Edward (ed.): *A House of Kings: The History of Westminster Abbey*, John Baker, 1966
*Catechism of the Catholic Church*, Continuum, 1994
Eeles, Francis C.: *The Coronation Service in Memory and History*, Mowbray, 1952
Fowke, Frank Rede: *The Bayeux Tapestry*, Arundel Society, 1875
Luard, Henry Richards: *Lives of Edward the Confessor*, Longman, Brown, Green, Longmans, and Roberts, 1858
Stenton, Frank: *Anglo-Saxon England*, Oxford, 1989
William of Malmesbury, *Chronicle of the Kings of England*, Perennial, 2016

Thomas Becket

Barlow, Frank: *Thomas Becket*, Weidenfeld and Nicholson, 1986
Evans, G.R.: *Saint Anselm of Canterbury*, Continuum, 1989

Greenaway, George (ed.): *The Life and Death of Thomas Becket*, Folio, 1961
Guy, John: *Thomas Becket*, Viking, 2012
Staunton, Michael (ed.): *The Lives of Thomas Becket*, Manchester University Press, 2001

Thomas More

Bolt, Robert: *A Man for All Seasons*, Heinemann, 1983
Guy, John: *Thomas More*, Arnold, 2000
Guy, John: *Tudor England*, Oxford, 1990
Logan, George M.: *The Cambridge Companion to Thomas More*, Cambridge, 2011
Marius, Richard: *Thomas More*, Fount, 1986
More, Thomas: *Utopia*, Penguin, 2012
Reynolds, E.E.: *Margaret Roper, Eldest Daughter of St Thomas More*, Burns & Oates, 1960
Roper, William and Harpsfield, Nicholas: *Lives of Saint Thomas More*, Dent, 1963
Rowse, A.L. (ed.): *A Man of Singular Virtue*, Folio Society, 1980